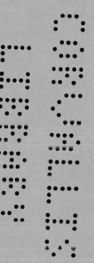

Souls in the Hands
of a Tender God

SOULS IN THE HANDS OF A TENDER GOD

Stories of the Search for Home and Healing on the Streets

CRAIG RENNEBOHM
WITH DAVID PAUL

BEACON PRESS

Boston

BEACON PRESS
25 Beacon Street
Boston, Massachusetts 02108-2892
www.beacon.org

Beacon Press books
are published under the auspices of
the Unitarian Universalist Association of Congregations.

11 10 09 08   8 7 6 5 4 3 2 1

This book is printed on acid-free paper that meets the uncoated paper
ANSI/NISO specifications for permanence as revised in 1992.

Composition by Wilsted & Taylor Publishing Services

Rennebohm, Craig
   Souls in the hands of a tender God : stories of the search for home and healing on the streets /
by Craig Rennebohm with David Paul.
      p. cm.
   ISBN 978-0-8070-0042-7
   1. Mental health—Religious aspects—Christianity. 2. Spiritual healing. 3. Mental illness—
Religious aspects—Christianity. 4. Healing—Religious aspects—Christianity. 5. Suffering—
Religious aspects—Christianity. 6. Spiritual biography. I. Paul, David W. II. Title.

   BT732.4.R46 2008
   242—dc22   2007031506

TO BARB

CONTENTS

Preface

Each of us has a story, and deep within our stories is a spiritual movement. Our life journeys sometimes take us through times of struggle, when we most need the resources of our faith in order to heal and find wholeness. It is especially at these times that we confront the deepest truths about what it means to be human.

Souls in the Hands of a Tender God begins with stories from the street, stories that describe the experience of mental illness, stories from more than thirty years of ministry with people who have been on the edges of life. These are stories of struggle and recovery, suffering and hope. In them we discover the movement of the Spirit, the touch of the Holy, the infinite tenderness of God. The stories illuminate who we are as persons, what it means to live in community, and how we are all ultimately connected in a universe of intimate and loving support.

This book is about the pilgrimage of healing and the importance of companionship in the journey out of suffering. And it is about all of us—those of us who are experiencing, or have experienced, mental illness, and those of us who are called to share the burden with family members, friends, and neighbors who are fighting for recovery. On the way together toward health, we are invited to meet at the most basic level, as human beings, called to be present with one another, to listen and hold one another in care.

Some may feel uncomfortable reading about the circumstances of the people in these stories. Perhaps it is because, deep within, we recognize that illness is never far from any one of us. Serious mental illness such as depression, bipolar disorder, or schizophrenia strikes approximately one in ten of us. One in four families has a loved one facing serious mental illness. The numbers are large, and the reality exists in our midst.

There is hope, however, amid the struggle. *Souls in the Hands of a Tender God* tells of people, once lost in episodes of mental illness and existing on the edges of life, who have found their way off the street to recovery and stability. Each story is rooted in a real person. To preserve the confidentiality of the persons on whom the narratives focus—the people from the street and others with whom Craig has ministered—we have changed details of name, setting, and personal descriptions. In some cases, we have blended several stories into one. However, we use the actual names of professional colleagues with whom Craig works. The "I" in the book's first-person narrative is Chaplain Craig Rennebohm of Seattle, Washington, who has been present as the stories unfolded.

These are intimate stories of personal courage and triumph, but they are also parables providing wisdom about faith, community, and the healing sciences, encouraging us to explore the spiritual dimensions of brain disorders and to see the healing process as a pilgrimage in which we, as a community, all have a part.

The struggle cries out for community action to make amends for a missed opportunity. In 1963 the United States Congress passed the Community Mental Health Act, which envisioned a network of care across this country to support citizens who were being discharged from an antiquated state hospital system. That promise has not been fulfilled, and the vision of community care remains unrealized. While great strides have been made in science and the treatment of brain disorders, we have never put in place the full complement of clinics and housing needed to care adequately for all who face mental illness. The numbers of people wandering untreated on our streets, wasting away in jails without proper care, and waiting with desperate families for assistance, bear witness to a core responsibility that we, in our common life, have not yet lived up to.

Within our culture, mental illness is still shrouded in stigma and misunderstanding. It has low priority in the arena of public policy, and it is a topic rarely addressed in our congregations and seminaries. In our faith communities, the average layperson and many clergy —even those specially trained in pastoral care and counseling—do not feel equipped to deal with the problem.

The authors hope this book will contribute to the movement to change the way our culture, and especially our faith communities, think about brain disorders and those who are afflicted. We hope the stories in these pages will help demystify mental illness and encourage efforts to build communities of openness, understanding, and care, with active participation and leadership from local congregations.

As we write, we build on the efforts of colleagues in the ministry, such as the late Stewart D. Govig, who wrote about mental illness in his family; Father Patrick Howell, who has written about his own struggle with psychosis; and Susan Gregg-Schroeder, who has written about her struggle with depression. In particular, our work has roots in that of Anton Boisen (1876–1965), a chaplain who served at the Worcester State Hospital in Massachusetts, where he himself had been a patient, and later at Elgin State Hospital in Illinois. Boisen sought to understand mental illness and healing in dialogue with the medical and psychological knowledge of his day, and he worked to shape a spiritual wisdom and pastoral care supportive of recovery and well-being.

Boisen's work has inspired our efforts to address both the spiritual dimensions and the scientific aspects of healing. Writing of a loving God and a Spirit of healing that operates within and among us, we invite our readers to a dialogue—a discussion we hope will engage people from a wide range of religious and spiritual backgrounds. At the same time, we affirm and give thanks for the gifts that science and medicine bring to the process of healing. Skilled diagnosis; basic research; the development of new and more effective medications; proven practices of outreach, care, and counseling; and a growing commitment to maximize each person's recovery—all of these factors provide concrete hope now and for the future.

Faith opens us to a spiritual power, a deeper vision of who we are, and an awareness of the larger purpose of our existence—all vital to our healing and quest for wholeness. The healing arts and sciences attend to the physical and emotional aspects of our lives, to how we perceive and think, to how our brains and minds work and are shaped as we grow and share in the world with others. Just as readers are encouraged to seek spiritual support and guidance to help them through their own illness or that of a loved one, the authors also urge readers to consult appropriate care providers about any questions concerning diagnosis and treatment. It is our view that faith and science, spiritual care and medicine, complement each other in fostering wellness.

The stories that follow are, in the end, a statement of faith. Illness raises the question of where our lives ultimately rest, and where we find love and care adequate to our fragility. We are each held with extraordinary gentleness in the hands of a tender God.

Craig Rennebohm and David Paul

A Note on Scriptures

When I was nine, I received a Revised Standard Version (RSV) of the Bible, presented to me by the Sunday school of Luther Memorial Church in Madison, Wisconsin. I have continued to use that Bible for more than fifty years. When I was ordained in 1970, my parents gave me a copy of the New Jerusalem Bible (NJB). Joseph Blenkinsopp, my Hebrew Testament professor at the Chicago Theological Seminary, served on the editorial committee for this version of the Scriptures, widely used in the Roman Catholic community. The NJB is a translation of a biblical text tradition that includes the books of Judith, Tobit, Wisdom, Ecclesiasticus, and Maccabees I and II. I have found both the RSV and the NJB helpful in the formation of my faith and ministry, and these are the versions we have used for citations in this book.

Craig Rennebohm

Prologue

A man dashes down the hillside toward the lakeshore. He has no clothes on, and his body is caked with dirt. His hair is a tangled mess, and his wrists and ankles are bound by iron manacles and chains that he has broken. He lives in the local cemetery, isolated from the community of the living.

Now he appears on the scene, crying out in confusion, just as Jesus steps out of a boat to address the Gerasenes. The crowd parts and scatters as the man approaches, but Jesus waits calmly, his arms at his sides, his hands held open. The teacher summons the Spirit of peace and healing within himself, and greets the man with grace and gentleness, honoring his soul, his whole being, his illness and his potential for health, his suffering and his sacredness.

The man falls to the ground, questioning Jesus loudly and begging not to be tormented.

Jesus asks him, "What is your name?"

"Legion," he says, for he is plagued by many voices in his head. He stands as if on the edge of an abyss, in great fear and terror. The voices beg to be let go.

Jesus gives the voices leave to go.

The people who had scattered slowly return. To their surprise, they find the man sitting with Jesus, clothed and in his right mind.

Adapted from Mark 5 and Luke 8:26–36

PART I

The Movement of the Spirit

In the first verse of the Bible, we read that God created the heavens and the earth. In the second verse, we read that the Spirit of God is "moving," giving life and shape and form to the world. That selfsame Spirit, the *breath of God* that gives life; the Spirit that animated the prophets and is the power of love and mercy embodied in Jesus—that Spirit is active as Comforter and Counselor to us each in every generation, and in every condition of our lives, including illness, confusion, and despair.

Part I of this book invites you into the experience of mental illness, life as it is when our moods and thoughts are deeply disturbed and we find ourselves on the margins of existence. We begin not in the sanctuary, but on the street. Here in the most unexpected and obscure places, we discover the Spirit at work in the world, the *touch of God* that holds every moment of life with infinite care.

I

AT THE DOORWAY

Pilgrim Church in Seattle has a chapel with a small courtyard opening through an archway onto a side street, and one morning as I was passing by on my way into the building, I noticed four bags of garbage, one at each corner of the courtyard. At the doorway to the chapel itself, protected from the rain, a man was sleeping. He awoke and raised his head as I approached. I said my name was Craig and that I was the pastor. He told me he was a baker and that he spent the nights baking bread for the whole city. He shot constant glances over my shoulder, his eyes scanning the courtyard.

He said there was a great evil in the world; he had put the bags of garbage out to protect himself and the church. I moved closer and crouched down to listen more carefully.

"The evil goes to what it knows," he said.

I asked his name.

"Sterling Hayden," he said, "the actor." He was referring to the movie star whose career had peaked in the 1950s, some twenty years earlier.

It was November, a season of ever-colder weather, but Sterling continued to sleep in the chapel courtyard, exposed to the night air. Each morning for a week I found him there, bags of garbage carefully set out around him to ward off the evil. Each morning we talked a little. Each morning the custodian carefully removed the garbage to the Dumpster. Each evening Sterling rebuilt his surround of safety.

One morning as we sat side by side on the steps leading from the street to the courtyard, a steady downpour began. I invited him inside. We climbed the stairs of the parish house to my study, a room with an old rolltop desk and a simple sitting area with comfortable chairs. Sterling confided to me how worried he was. Unnameable threats hovered about him. He lapsed into silence, an inner world of terror showing through frightened eyes.

What I first saw in Sterling was his "illness self"—the homeless man, his strange sense of identity, his terrible fright, his unusual attempts to create safety. As we sat together over the course of that week, there were also brief and fleeting moments of ordinary conversation and health. He asked for a drink of water. He gently touched a small green plant growing on the windowsill.

On his last night with us, Sterling placed large amounts of toxics around the courtyard. The next morning, in one corner we found a box of used motor-oil cans and dirty rags scavenged from a gas station. In another corner was a five-gallon bucket of old cooking grease hauled from the alley behind a nearby restaurant. In a third corner was a bag of half-filled bottles and spray cans of cleansers. In the fourth corner sat a carton of empty containers that once held paint thinner, shellac, and wood stain. These materials were the only protection Sterling could devise.

When I saw Sterling's volatile collection in the courtyard, I talked with him about going to the hospital. I said he might find safety and care there. The hospital, I told him, protected people from disease and infection. They had good security and staff on duty day and night, help that we didn't have at the church. I told him there was a team that could come and help him. To my relief, he was willing.

I called King County Mental Health Crisis and Commitment Services, and was told that county-designated mental health professionals (MHPs) would be dispatched promptly. Sterling and I waited in my office, and after about thirty minutes two men arrived. They listened to Sterling's frightened and confused story. The MHPs agreed that he needed help and should be in the hospital.

Sterling relaxed a little. "Can we go now?" he asked. "Will you take me?"

The MHPs looked at each other, then at me, and then at Sterling. "Sterling," one of them said, "we can't do that. We can only take people to the hospital if they don't want to go."

Sterling looked crushed, and I was incredulous.

"He wants to go," I said. "Why can't you take him?"

"Sterling is a voluntary patient," one of the MHPs replied. "We can only arrange transportation for *involuntary* patients, people we're committing to the hospital against their will."

I shook my head. This was absurd.

Before I could put together a question about what we could do, Sterling shouted at me, "You said these people would help!" and dashed out of the room.

"Sterling, wait!" I called. I wanted to ask the MHPs if I could take him, and to which hospital, and whom we should talk to. I hadn't a clue how to get someone into a psychiatric unit in Seattle.

Sterling bolted down the stairs and out the back door. I assumed he would head for his haven in the chapel courtyard, and so before pursuing him I hurriedly got some suggestions from the MHPs. After they left, I went to look for Sterling. He wasn't in the courtyard. I looked on Broadway, the street in front of the church, and in the nearby neighborhood, but he had vanished.

I watched for him over the next several days, but he never returned.

Just before Thanksgiving, several weeks after Sterling disappeared, I was reading the *Seattle Times*. At the bottom of a back-page column was a paragraph of filler. A transient had been found under a viaduct downtown, dead from exposure. His name was Sterling Hayden.

The experience with Sterling was a beginning, coming early on in my ministry with Pilgrim Church. Pilgrim stood on the corner of Broadway, in the middle of a diverse and ever-changing neighborhood just beyond Seattle's downtown core. The needs of our neighbors and the makeup of our congregation offered a ready calling to mission.

Among us were elderly individuals and couples on fixed incomes, students, street people, young professional families and families on assistance, young adults, and people from a wide variety of ethnic and religious backgrounds. We sought to diminish the barriers that discouraged or excluded anybody from participating in the life of our community of faith by ramping the front entrance for wheelchair access, signing the Sunday services for the deaf and hard of hearing, and printing the hymnal and weekly service bulletin in braille. Residents from nearby group homes became members of the church, and we did our best with anyone who came in on a Sunday morning acting out of the ordinary.

We hosted a community meal we called the Lord's Supper, where served and servers prepared and ate dinner together. We used an old locker/shower facility in the basement to create the "Lower Room," named by the street community and staff in reference to the Upper Room where Jesus met with his disciples. Here was a practical but also sacred place, a down-to-earth starting point for a new journey. We replumbed the showers, put in a laundry, and stocked the shelves with clothes and supplies for people who were homeless or hungry. The Lower Room became a center of support and fellowship, as well as a base for opening another space for emergency shelter in cold weather.

We discovered, however, that there were neighbors who could not make it to our doors—people who were too hopeless, too gripped by delusional fears, or too caught up in mania: minds too confused, souls too wounded to find their way into survival services. And even when they found us, we were often unprepared as a congregation for ministering with them. Out front, our reader board proclaimed, "All are welcome, come as you are," but our ability to put that bold and basic principle into practice had a serious limitation when it came to the nearly 10 percent among us who are afflicted with major depression, bipolar disorder, schizophrenia, or other severe mental illnesses.

It was not just the congregation; I was unprepared to help a person like Sterling. Sterling had brought his struggle to our doorstep, and I had responded to the best of my ability. We began with hesitation on both sides of the relationship. Sterling had tried to tell his story as clearly as he could from out of the ominous clouds of his illness, and I attempted to listen and find the path with him toward healing. We took a few trusting steps, but lost our way. Why?

I had a background in counseling, but no real understanding of brain disorders. In seminary, I had taken the basic pastoral care class, but during the course only one sentence was spoken that specifically addressed major mental illness: "A person with mental illness should be referred to a psychiatrist." In our seminaries and churches, as in the wider culture, mental illness was shrouded in myth and stigma. Care and treatment were a mystery.

Sterling's story was tragic, a painful memory that slipped into a forgotten recess of my mind, only to be awakened several years later. In the meantime, I had left the parish ministry for a year of study at the Pacific School of Religion in Berkeley, California, and I began the program with an intensive summer of clinical pastoral education. In that capacity, I was assigned as a chaplain to a psychiatric unit of a county hospital. After a brief introduction to the unit and its staff and patients, I was given a key to the ward and told to make sure that the door was always locked behind me.

It was an eye-opening experience. One man sat in the dayroom muttering, "No hope, no hope." Another wandered about the halls, stringing together words that seemingly made no sense: "Debt, debt, debt, everyone's in debt, gas, got to get the glover in, got to get the glover in, no, no, no glover, everything goes boom." A young woman talked rapidly about a book she was writing, which would contain everything a person needed to know about any subject, "all the wisdom of the world, a superbible." One day a man ran down the hall and slammed his head into a door.

Slowly I got to know each of these souls, along with dozens of others who came through the unit over the summer. My approach to them was simple: I introduced myself as a fellow human being, a neighbor, and offered to be present. It wasn't clear to me what help I could be, but I was willing to learn from the patients and staff. I looked for small ways to create islands of safety, little spaces of sanctuary where the patients and I could sit quietly side by side, or stand, or just walk a few steps together. I listened to people's stories, in whatever way they were able to share them with me. I participated with patients in group art activities, in singing together, and in activities involving movement and drama. If asked, I joined patients when they met with their psychiatrist or other staff. I said goodbye as patients left the unit, some heading back to their families, some to group homes and other facilities, and some to the streets.

One afternoon I was called to the emergency room. Franklin, a patient who had been discharged that morning, had returned. With nowhere to go that night, he begged to be readmitted and was so agitated that he had to be strapped down on a gurney. He asked to talk with the chaplain. When I found him, he was still lying on the gurney as staff evaluated his condition and made a decision concerning the disposition of his case.

Franklin saw me enter the room. He reached for my hand and said, "Tell me, please, that someone cares."

I thought of Sterling and recalled my sense of helplessness when he bolted from my office and disappeared. What could I tell the man here before me now? I couldn't guarantee him anything, but I could minister to him. I could share with him what I most deeply believed.

I took Franklin's hand. "Someone cares," I said. "Someone cares."

He nodded, lay back, and rested.

In the space between us, we sensed the tenderness of God, holding us in quietude and patience, a Spirit active even when our lives are broken. The healing touch of God is manifest in the times of our greatest vulnerability and when our relationships with one another are fragile. God is there for us when we reach the precipice. When we feel helpless, when we are all too conscious of our failures, when we have done all we can and it is not enough, when we feel overcome by destructive forces at work in us and in the world, when we stand at the abyss . . . it is then that we experience the touch of God: an aged, veined hand that reaches out to soothe us, support us, and anoint us with love and life.

This is faith: to experience a spirit of assurance transcending all that is negative, destructive, and alienating. This is faith: to know that, whatever our condition, no matter who we are or what we have done, no matter how overwhelming the forces working within us or upon us, there is One who cares for us and dwells with us and holds us with an infinitely tender strength, One who is pained by our pain and passionate about our healing and well-being. This is faith: to feel, to comprehend, to be touched by the presence of divine love in a moment of shared clarity. The gentleness of God creates room for us to be present with one another and to discover in depth who we are and what it means to be human.

We are pilgrims. Some of us travel familiar roads throughout our lives, highways well marked; we might never leave the village or neighborhood in which we grow up. Others of us move out into new territories, different and distant lands, to follow our calling or our dreams. And some of us are taken, not of our own will or choice, into the landscapes of illness. But wherever we are on the journey, we are on holy ground. Our lives are sacred—and no less so when our brains are in disorder. God holds our souls and walks with us.

Out of the experience with Franklin and other patients, a new ministry emerged for me. I had gone to Berkeley with the idea of pursuing peace work, but what I began to realize was that the work of peacemaking, the work of healing and reconciliation, was literally on our doorstep. Our first calling is to create communities that care for and include the most fragile, vulnerable, and estranged among us. In reaching out to the stranger in our own midst, the person we have been taught to fear or ignore or shun or despise, we discover the fundamentals of faith. The pilgrimage of peace does not require travel to faraway sites; the way begins with our next step, with our neighbor who is suffering.

In June of 1987, I returned from Berkeley to Seattle and started the Mental Health Chaplaincy, a ministry that took me into the streets to share the journey with people like Sterling and Franklin.

Soon after arriving back in Seattle, I met Terri. Terri lived on the streets of Seattle's First Hill. Each night she passed by St. James

Cathedral, a stately, Italian Renaissance–style church on First Hill overlooking downtown, with a warm and open ministry especially for those who are on the margins. Terri often stopped and took up a post by the main entrance or a side door, sheltered as much as possible from the wind and the cold. When others came seeking sanctuary, she helped them find a place, too. Those who were troublemakers she asked to leave. "This is holy ground," she said with determination, standing at her full height of four feet, five inches. On the stormiest nights, Terri found shelter in the emergency waiting area of a nearby hospital; she had once worked there and knew the security staff and maintenance personnel.

During the day, Terri helped out in the cathedral sanctuary, volunteering for small duties such as polishing the pews or replacing the candles. She loved the daily services at eight, noon, and five, which to her were like the hours prayed in medieval abbeys and monasteries.

Terri lived with two neurological illnesses. She needed medication to control seizures, which had plagued her since childhood. She also suffered from tuberous sclerosis (TS), a rare genetic disorder that causes growths to appear spontaneously throughout the body. Terri had experienced episodes of disfiguring growths on both her hands and face.

Despite these impediments, she maintained steady employment and raised a developmentally disabled son, who moved into supported living as an adult. Terri quit work and gave up her apartment to assist her mother, an invalid, in the family home. When Terri's mother was transferred to a nursing facility, the house was sold to help pay for the cost of her care. Terri stayed with friends for a while, but then, insisting that she did not want to be a burden, she drifted out onto the streets.

With no income and bereft of daily contact with the two people she loved most, Terri did her best to create a meaningful world on the street. She saw herself as a kind of Saint Francis. Money given to her she would pass on to others. Food and other material mercies that came her way were always shared. Terri initially viewed her homelessness as a call and a test of her faith that God would provide. She cherished two small candles of hope in her life. She had once served as the day housekeeper and cook in a rectory far out in the country and wished very much to be of service in this way at the cathedral, but no such position was available. Above all, Terri desired to become a eucharistic minister, a layperson in the Roman Catholic Church trained and authorized to assist at the altar in serving Holy Communion. For that to happen, she needed more stability in her life.

The cathedral staff were touched by Terri's devotion and concerned about her health and well-being. Terri had had several seizures during services but refused the emergency medical technicians' offer to take her to the hospital. She was no longer taking her seizure medication, and she hadn't had an evaluation of her TS for several years.

Sister Anne, who knew Terri well, called me to ask if I would meet with Terri and see if there was anything I could do to help her. The three of us had a quiet conversation in the ornate rectory parlor. I was struck by Terri's challenges, her sensitivity and tenacity, and the range and depth of her faith journey. She admitted that she was lonely but said that a lot of people on the street had no one. She acknowledged her seizures and the TS but pointed out that others on the street suffered as much or more. Terri told us that occasionally one of the women in the lay Carmelite community she belonged to would take her in. Sister Anne assured Terri of the cathedral staff's concern, as well as their desire to help her find stability and become more fully part of the community.

A part of Terri genuinely wanted to find her way off the street, but a part of her was afraid to make a change. I could see her soul struggle as her eyes focused and then went vacant. Her hands opened, then closed; reached out, then pulled back; were calm, then twisted. At one point she hugged herself, as if in an effort to hold everything together. She felt she had enough strength to stay with what she knew out on the street, and she preferred that over the uncertainty posed by change.

As someone new to Terri, I did not push her. I asked her if it was okay to say hello when I saw her on my rounds, and suggested that we might have a cup of coffee or tea and talk again. She smiled and nodded. In the weeks to come, we developed a connection, talking from time to time on the sidewalk. She wanted to share with me her view of life without a home, and she introduced me to others who needed help. She encouraged me to give them a hand but declined any aid for herself.

Terri trusted in God to help. A coin found on the sidewalk was a sign of providence. A bag of food left on the cathedral steps was evidence of grace. She ate once a day at the Family Kitchen, run by the Catholic Worker community. She helped serve and clean up, and she welcomed others.

But then her behavior began to change. At mass, she would leave her place in the congregation, walk up to the altar, and position herself to help serve the Communion elements. Sister Anne or an usher would gently help her back to a pew, for she had not been trained to serve Communion. She began having difficulty tracking conversations and following instructions. Her memory was faulty, and she seemed increasingly detached or despondent; hopelessness, worry, and guilt were sapping her strength. She showed signs of a growing depression. She was less and less herself, this tiny, normally energetic, street-savvy, self-appointed guardian of the cathedral steps. What had once been offbeat, eccentric thinking was now increasingly strange and disturbing, even to Terri. She believed she was constantly followed. She said she heard people talking about her in whispered conversations on the bus, in the city library, and at the cathedral. She was having trouble sleeping. She no longer had much appetite and stopped taking part in the community meal. She grew gradually weaker. Several of the staff she most trusted sought to help her reconnect with her doctors, but Terri insisted that she did not need assistance.

Early one afternoon, Terri, Sister Anne, and I reconvened in the rectory parlor. We sat in the dignified comfort of three old upholstered chairs and watched a steady downpour of rain outside the window.

"I've done my best," Terri said quietly.

"We know you have, Terri," I said. "It's not easy." I paused, knowing that what I was about to propose was something she had not been willing to consider up to now.

"I have a friend in the walk-in clinic," I said, pointing up the street in the direction of the Harborview Medical Center. "I would love to have you meet her. She's like Sister Anne and me, someone who could be part of your team, someone who could help us."

I waited, letting the notion rest in the space between us.

"I don't know," said Terri. "I don't want to be a burden."

"I know you don't," I said. I could feel her struggling against admitting her need for help.

"Terri," I said, "you look very tired and sad. I think it would help to get checked out, maybe get some good rest, get stronger again."

We sat in quiet, resting once more on that holy ground which Terri had told so many others was there to support *them*.

"Terri," I said, "let's just take a walk up to the chaplain's office at the hospital. You can see where the walk-in clinic is."

Terri agreed. On the way into the main hospital, we passed the entrance to the mental health center, which housed the only clinic in the county where a person could walk in and get a brief, initial assessment of serious mental health issues that day. Terri stopped and looked, but she didn't want to go in.

We made our way to a small meditation room near the Spiritual Care Department offices. We sat quietly for a time. Then we talked a little more. Terri began to cry softly. Gently I touched her hand.

"Terri," I said softly, "come with me."

Terri took a deep breath and slowly stood up. She looked at me, not so much making a conscious choice but waiting for some deeper movement within her, or between us. I prayed that we might be able to go forward and tried as best I could to keep the way ahead clear.

I looked at Terri and held my hand out toward the door. We took a step together and then kept walking.

We returned to the walk-in clinic. I held the door open and stood at the counter where patients write their names and time of arrival on the sign-in sheet. We waited together until the receptionist called Terri and took down her basic personal information—name, date of birth, Social Security number, address (homeless), next of kin (mother in a nursing home), insurance (none), income (none), current health provider (none). Terri was asked to read and sign two legal documents, a patient's rights form and a consent-for-treatment form. She asked me what they meant. She was at the brink again, and I could sense that this might be too much, the signing of these papers. We talked about her right to get help, to ask questions, to be treated with respect and dignity. We talked about the staff's need to have her permission to visit with her and offer her care.

Slowly, she signed the two documents. We returned to the waiting room. A financial worker called her name, and we went into a small office. A kindly woman explained that because Terri had no income, she would qualify for subsidized care that morning. She just needed to answer a few questions so the clinic could be reimbursed. Terri responded to another series of inquiries about bank accounts, other assets, work, and eligibility for various benefit programs; she signed another form and listened as the financial worker explained that she could apply for public assistance.

Terri again looked at me, shaking her head and mouthing, "I don't want to do this."

The interview was over. I nodded in understanding and said, "Let's go back to the waiting room and let things settle for a minute. You've done everything you need to do for now. We can talk to Jane"—the colleague we were waiting to see—"and then we'll just take it from there. You are really doing well. I appreciate how hard this is, but you're doing well."

A few minutes later, Jane came out. She introduced herself and invited us back to her desk. She told Terri that she had some questions she needed to ask; some would be personal, and some might seem strange. She wanted Terri to let her know if anything made her uncomfortable. She invited Terri to ask questions, too. "I'm glad you've come in," Jane said.

Terri relaxed a little and began to respond. Jane listened to her with empathy and spoke compassionately. She suggested several possible courses of action but gently recommended that Terri come into the hospital. Patiently, Jane addressed Terri's worries and explained why the hospital would be the most helpful choice. Jane was sensitive to Terri's words, her voice, and she replied in language Terri herself used and found comforting. Still, Terri was ambivalent. She agreed tentatively. Jane reassured her that it was a difficult but good decision, framing the choice in a way that affirmed who Terri was, both in her struggles and in her strengths. She then arranged for Terri to be admitted to the hospital.

Terri and I crossed the street to the admitting office, and I accompanied her to the floor. We said goodbye, and I assured her I would be back to see her again the next day.

In the hospital, Terri received a thorough workup. Medications were prescribed to help with her depression and fearfulness. She participated in a variety of educational and counseling groups. A social worker assisted her in developing a discharge plan that included outpatient care and steps aimed at getting her into stable housing. The medical team encouraged her to work with her former internist and neurologist to attend to the seizure disorder and to a recurrence of the tuberous sclerosis.

Thereafter, a psychiatrist and case manager met regularly with Terri. The doctor listened and answered her questions with patience, engaging her ups and downs in mood and carefully exploring her thoughts and ideas. They discussed the side effects of her medications and adjusted the prescriptions as needed. The case manager helped Terri find shelter and transitional housing, went shopping with her, helped her coordinate appointments with other caregivers, and assisted her in getting a bus pass and negotiating applications for public assistance, Supplemental Security Income, and health benefits.

In this way, a circle of care formed around Terri. A growing number of people were available to help her with specific aspects of her life—something we all need. Terri renewed old friendships. She became active in the life of the cathedral as she had been in the past, developing a new sense of mutuality and belonging.

Terri and I continued to meet regularly. In many ways the journey for us had just begun. Our conversations focused increasingly on matters of faith. For Terri, as it is for many of us, healing was a process not only of restoring well-being but also of personal renewal, a process of reintegrating fragmented selves, of salvation in the fullest sense of the word. Out of the crisis of illness, Terri discovered more fully and deeply who she was.

After several months in a shelter and transitional housing, Terri made a move that absolutely delighted her. Paul, the housing coordinator at the mental health center, had an apartment for her. A smile burst across Terri's face as she recognized the address, kitty-corner across from the cathedral, in a building where she had lived some years before. Several of us helped her find furnishings for her new home. One afternoon we shopped together at a used-furniture store, where Terri picked out a solid round table and four chairs. "I'm planning to have guests, you know." The next day Father Ryan, the pastor of the cathedral, and I sat with Terri at what she now proudly called her "ecumenical table," sharing the blessing of this welcome home.

Once a week, Terri made sandwiches for the men's shelter at St. James. She continued her volunteer duties in the sanctuary and arranged for her son to join her each weekend for mass and a visit.

One day she placed a book in my hands, Teresa of Ávila's *Interior Castle*—a surprise gift. Terri was widely read in Catholic spiritual writings, both classical and contemporary, and Saint Teresa was one of her favorites. During several visits, we discussed Saint Teresa's idea that in our minds are many rooms out of which we live, and that we all have an ultimate home in the heart of God. On another occasion, Terri introduced me to the writings of Anthony de Mello, a Jesuit from India who developed a creative blend of Eastern and traditional Christian spiritual exercises. Yet another work that Terri shared with me was Thérèse of Lisieux's autobiography, *The Story of a Soul*, in which Saint Thérèse described her "little way" of manifesting love for God through small acts of service to the community.

Terri found great comfort in these books. In the words, she found wisdom and encouragement. In the writers and their journeys, she found models and guides. In their prayers and practice, she discovered encouragement to shape her own spiritual path and grow her soul.

And eventually, Terri realized one of her longtime dreams. Sister Claudette invited her to begin training as a eucharistic minister. On the night of her investiture I sat in the congregation, watching as Terri, white-robed and beaming, gently and confidently helped distribute the bread and cup of Communion. In her and with her and through her, the gifts of God's presence and love became real and shared with others.

In an important sense, Sterling and Terri's stories are our stories, whoever we are. We are all vulnerable. All of us suffer. We may be suffering now; we may have suffered in the past or will suffer in the future—not all of us from brain disorders, thankfully, but from one or many physical illnesses or maladies of the soul. Our illness self—the face and persona reflecting that which afflicts us—may predominate at any given moment, but it is not absolute and does not determine finally who we are. An illness, no matter how grave, is but a part of our larger identity; our wholeness as persons encompasses the moments of illness and far more. Healing is the ultimate frame in which we live. Healing does not merely treat the disturbances within and among us. Healing recognizes our strengths and gifts and seeks to include illness within a larger frame of personal growth and caring community. Healing honors the essential worth and dignity of us each. Healing holds us open to our greatest potential and proceeds from an infinite horizon of high purpose and eternal possibility. Healing flows from the ultimate tenderness that is at the heart of life.

Sterling's story illustrates how fragile the thread of life can be. His story calls us to consider the effects of our ignorance and the fate of persons in a world where the inns of welcome and healing are far too few for the many in need. Sterling's story leaves us fallen grievously short, grasping for meaning.

Like Sterling, Terri walked perilously close to the edge; she, too, might have disappeared from among us. Her story speaks to us of struggle, but it also illustrates the power of a community to care. Her story reminds us of the gifts we have to help each other. Terri's story offers hope.

2

JERRY'S SONG

In the old district of downtown Seattle, down a flight of stairs from sidewalk level, around a couple turns and through a door, is a service center. Hispanics who live on the street call it the *Hoyo,* the Hole, because of its subterranean location, but it's not a hole-in-the-wall or a pit. As we enter, we see a large, low-ceilinged space filled with tables. Near the front door is a service counter where people can get a pair of shoes, a clean shirt, or a jacket; or they can sign up for a shower in an adjacent room and borrow a towel. Some seventy or eighty people of various races and ages, mostly men, sit around the tables, and there's an ongoing murmur of conversation. One man sleeps, his head cradled in his arms on a tabletop. Several have sleeping bags rolled up or piled next to their chairs. In a corner of the room, a card game is in progress. Before the city banned smoking in public interiors, the place used to be bathed in a gray-brown haze, but otherwise the atmosphere was one of simplicity and warmth, as it still is. The center was, and is, a kind of club, and some of the folks who eventually find a home return to help those who are still left behind. One feels welcome here.

It was here that I first met Jerry, seated on a folding chair at a table and sipping coffee from an old chipped mug. He had on a tattered dress shirt with frayed cuffs under the stained and rumpled sport coat that he had once, long ago, worn to work—a sign of a professional man who cared about his appearance, back in the days when he was able to maintain it. He was then, from all accounts, a modest, competent, and thoughtful citizen.

Since then, however, illness had kindled in Jerry and he had developed a reputation of another sort. Service staffers knew him as one of the most difficult individuals on the street. One day he would bluster about the city, claiming to be the commandant of the coast guard; the next, he was the superintendent of construction for all downtown buildings; on another day, he was the Treasurer of the United States. In the midst of these episodes Jerry was impatient and irritable, oblivious of the usual rules and regulations. He would shove to the front of the food line, berate shelter volunteers, and shout at service center staff. When his illness was full blown, he had little or no consciousness of his behavior. The quiet, caring, thoughtful man disappeared behind the symptoms of mania and grandiosity.

At various times Jerry's behavior got him barred from every shelter, drop-in center, and meal program in the city. There were days when he had literally nowhere to go. One morning I encountered him storming up out of the Hoyo. He headed grimly up the sidewalk, shaking and muttering. At first I followed him at a distance, but gradually I caught up with him, giving him berth, until at a corner we stood side by side. Jerry glanced my way, his eyes furious, and continued to stride forward. I stayed with him, and we walked together in silence for many blocks. Finally he slowed, and we turned into a small café. Still agitated, but somewhat calmer, Jerry sat and gazed at me. Eventually a tear formed in his eye. He shook his head. "Is there anything for me in this world?" he asked.

"There is, Jerry," I said. "There's something for each of us. Possibilities, purpose, potential."

On an afternoon a week or so later, the usual collection of people were in the Hoyo, trying on clothing at the service counter, drinking coffee, playing cards. At the rear counter, next to the coffee urn, volunteers were clearing away the pans and bowls from which they had just served a meal. Jerry suddenly began writing on the back of an old flyer that was on the table between us: where he was born; how he grew up; where he went to school; where he went to college; when he enlisted in the Navy; and when he worked.

Toward the bottom of the page, the pen moved faster and faster, and Jerry's writing began to sprawl. He pulled the pen back to the top of the sheet and continued his story, filling in the spaces between the lines. Reaching the bottom a second time, he wrote up the side of the paper and around the edges, then up and down the page across everything he had already written. Finally, in a furious rush, he scribbled sentences diagonally from one corner to the other. He spent about half an hour filling the paper with layers of dense, black ink that became nearly impossible to read.

Finished, he shoved the paper across the table.

"That's me," he said.

What I could read of Jerry's narrative revealed a complex pattern. It touched upon core events in his life—his childhood, his education, his time in the Navy—but the basic thread of his story was interrupted by tangents that he had added in bursts of emotion. Some of his story line had a dreamlike quality: he was making deliveries in a truck but then headed off on an imaginary journey that took him nowhere. He was riding a motorcycle along country roads, and then without any transition he was back home again. The pieces of his autobiography didn't fit together in any clear way.

Jerry's problems began while he was at sea, with what he characterized as a nervous breakdown following an incident in a storm off the Alaska coast. A radioman, he had been the only contact between his ship and a fishing vessel that was sinking. He relayed the messages coming from the distressed boat—its location, the condition of the crew, the calls for help—to the rescue command center. He stood in the gap, maintaining communication, receiving reports from the field, passing along the information for processing, and sending back action updates and encouragement. It was an exhausting and draining task, and Jerry gave his all.

Shortly after that ordeal, he experienced the first great storm of confusion in his mind. Jerry's brain, like yours and mine, is an intricate command and control system that had been called upon for complex tasks of information gathering, calculating, evaluating and making fast decisions, strategizing, three-way communicating, and giving moral support. All of these activities took place quickly and in an environment of intensified mood and emotion. Jerry's brain got him through the crisis, but then it malfunctioned. He slipped into repeated cycles of manic highs and miserable lows. When he first left the service, he was able to function professionally on the staff of a nonprofit organization, but eventually his illness overwhelmed him and drove him out of his career and into the streets.

For years, Jerry resisted any suggestion that he might be suffering from a mental disorder. Most of the people who crossed his path saw him only as a man who had lost touch with reality and couldn't control his anger. Few saw the process that had led to the full-blown presentation of Jerry's disorder. For those who wanted to help him—the service center staff, the well-intentioned volunteers—the best they could do was to contain Jerry's chaos, or confront it, or, in the end, give up trying to restrain him and ask him to leave. It's not that they were mean-spirited; they had difficulty understanding his illness and little training in how to help people like him.

What do people need when their brain chemistry is out of balance, when their thoughts and feelings are in disarray? They need a fellow human being who understands that what they are experiencing is serious, but treatable. They need both acceptance and honest responses, both sensitivity and clear, appropriate limits. They need someone who can help them get appropriate care from skilled practitioners who are trained to treat their particular form of illness. They need open doors to treatment and a continuum of care for long-term healing. Above all, they need the compassion and support of our communities, including especially our communities of faith.

Our society, our communities, and our culture are not adequately equipped for the scope of the task. Our congregations have not been prepared to care effectively for the multitude of brothers and sisters in our midst who suffer from mental illness. We haven't realized our potential for care, and we have created far too few possibilities for healing and growth.

We have only begun to grasp the wonderful complexity of the brain and to understand what is happening in the course of a brain disorder. The Bible offers a basic framework for appreciating the delicate and involved nature of our bodies and brains, but it doesn't begin to explain the actual composition and functioning of the cells and systems that make up the human being.

Each of us is a small universe of astonishing depth and richness, each of us a world worthy of exploration. The Psalmist reminds us that we are "intricately wrought," even before we emerge at birth (Ps. 139:15). Psalm 8:5 proclaims that we have been "created little less than God" and are "crowned with glory and honor." Thus the Psalmist, composing more than two millennia ago, sensed the outlines of the complexities and the potential in us. But of our specific physical, biological, and biochemical makeup, the Psalmist says little. It wasn't until more than two thousand years later that science began to identify the intricate molecular structures that constitute the human body.

And by far the most intricate part of our body is the brain, a crowning glory giving us the capacities to sense and feel, think, become unique persons in relation to others, and share together. It is the brain that enables us to have faith: to delve into life's mysteries and seek its deepest meanings.

Now, in the early years of the twenty-first century, science is just on the threshold of more fully understanding the complexity—and, indeed, the miracle of life—that is the human brain. Weighing less than three pounds, the brain contains hundreds of billions of cells, no two of which actually touch each other. Each cell is its own constantly shaping center of process and activity, joined in a surrounding sea as ships in a fleet, microscopic flotillas organizing to hold memory, give rise to mood and emotion, process sensations, carry language, create ideas and speech, imagine, choose, act and decide, write, draw, paint, sing and dance, believe, pray, and celebrate. In the mystery and complexity of the human brain lie the most mundane activities of monitoring our breathing and the beat of our hearts, as well as our capacity to experience the holy, what is ultimate and sacred.

Each of the hundreds of billions of cells in the brain is its own small miracle ship in a biochemical ocean. Every individual neuron has its own information-receiving system—up to ten thousand dendrites, receptor sites available to chemical messengers sent specifically from nearby cells, and a semipermeable cell wall open to the changing local waters, which bathe whole clusters of neighboring cells in common biochemical waves of informational activation, intensity, and modulation. Each individual brain cell also contains its own nucleus of activity, its own internal processing center, up to ten thousand protein molecules organizing and shaping and pulsing forth a unique contribution to our overall personal and human experience at any moment.

With so much activity going on all the time, it's no wonder that the brain can malfunction. Some of us are more fragile and vulnerable than others to subtle shifts in brain biochemistry, but under extremely violent or stressful conditions, any of us can be at risk for a breakdown in our ability to manage our emotions, think clearly, make decisions, communicate with others, or relate to even our dearest family members and friends.

Even in our daily lives, almost all of us have some experience of the extraordinary states of which the human brain is capable. Consider our dreams, the unusual, even bizarre, scenarios created in the midst of sleep; how we may awake and find ourselves unsure of where we are, disoriented in time and space and sense of self by the power of a nightmare or a dream. Consider our capacity for daydreams and fantasy, the power of the imagination. Consider the different interpretations we each can put on the same event.

Artists regularly demonstrate our capacity for experiencing and communicating the unusual, sometimes in quite strange and disturbing terms. The fluidity of the brain is an amazing gift.

When our friend Jerry was most ill, the disturbances within made it almost impossible for him to explore or even acknowledge his disorder. The very capacities we use to consider our situation, receive and process feedback from others, and choose a new direction—these are precisely what were impaired for Jerry. Nevertheless, something of Jerry's basic self, the self he and others knew when he was healthy—

what I call his *familiar self,* as distinct from his *illness self*—remained available and always potentially at hand, even in the worst moments of his internal storm and its external fury. We might walk miles together, Jerry fuming, I in silence, as the whirlwind spent itself and finally subsided. Sometimes the gusts and squalls came steadily and lasted for days, or dropped Jerry into extended depressions.

And for periods, he functioned with a relative wellness. He could be a model volunteer, a cooperative client at the shelter, a thoughtful and caring brother to others who were homeless. Jerry dearly wished to get off the street, but to do it on his own terms, not as a psychiatric patient. Such is the stigma associated with mental illness that few of us willingly embrace a diagnosis or readily accept treatment. Jerry was no exception. People from the service center staff had suggested treatment possibilities and attempted to get him into care. When his symptoms were full blown, he belligerently denied any need for help. When he was more coherent and available for conversation, he was wary and ambivalent about seeking mental healthcare. He questioned whether a doctor or drugs would do any good, and dredged up scenes from the movie *One Flew over the Cuckoo's Nest,* saying that he didn't want to end up somewhere with a Nurse Ratched, the cruel head nurse of the mental hospital portrayed in the film.

Jerry had a particularly intractable illness. He and I shared the journey together for seven lean years, building trust and understanding and making gradual connections with care. He loved people and genuinely enjoyed being with others. Eventually, he opened to the help of a young caseworker with the local affiliate of the National Health Care for the Homeless Council, Graydon, who began seeing him at a shelter he frequented. Graydon became a part of Jerry's team, and the three of us would meet over coffee or a sandwich. Graydon focused on practical issues and needs, helping Jerry negotiate reentry to the shelter when he faced a week's banishment, obtaining food stamps for him, helping him set up some basic routines, increasing his access to a clothing bank and showers, and assisting him when he eventually began applying for housing and benefits.

One day when he was feeling exhausted, Jerry agreed to go with us to the hospital. He saw it as a well-deserved R & R, rest and recuperation after his long struggle on the street. It was the right prescription for his battle fatigue, and he accepted it as such. Once on the inpatient unit, he watched carefully as others went about the healing process. The psychiatrist explored with him the possibility of medications. Jerry talked about his illness and paths to recovery with his hospital roommate, in group meetings, with other staff members, and on our visits together.

While Jerry was in the hospital, he asked me to bring him Communion. I arrived at his room with my kit, a box containing a wafer of bread and a small bottle of grape juice. I opened the box and set it on the bedside table. I broke the wafer in two and poured juice into two small Communion cups. I offered a prayer of blessing, and we shared the bread and the cup together.

"Would you bless the medicine if I took it?" he said.

"Sure," I said.

We celebrated two Communions that day, one of bread and juice, one of healing medicine—two sacred moments, two occasions of restoration, two moments of God's gift and grace.

About a year before Jerry got off the street, our community suffered a loss. Eddie, a staff member at the Hoyo, died of cancer. We set up the day center for a memorial service. Someone brought in flowers in small bottles to set on each of the round tables, and we fashioned an altar from a table at one end of the room. Refreshments were prepared. During the half hour before the service was to begin, people gathered. Eddie had worked at the center for a long time, and those who came to pay him tribute spanned several generations. There were ex-cons who had been among the first to populate the service center two and three decades earlier. There were middle-aged women who had fled, years ago, from abusive relationships. There were youthful runaways who were trying to escape violent home lives.

At the last moment, Jerry rushed in. Out of breath, he told me he wanted to say something at the memorial and then sing the "Bugle

Song." I wasn't sure what he had in mind, but I told him there would be a time for people to share their thoughts and memories. I invited him to speak if and when he felt ready. I didn't encourage the Bugle Song; the only thing that came to my mind was the Andrews Sisters singing their jazzy World War II tune, "The Boogie Woogie Bugle Boy."

The memorial service started with someone playing a Native American flute solo, a quiet, haunting, soothing sound. One of the regulars at the center read a poem she had written for the occasion, a tribute to Eddie and his many kindnesses to folks over the years. Elderly men, women long accustomed to life on the street, transients, persons struggling with mental illness and addictions—a roomful of the forgotten and troubled and barely making it—shared their stories of Eddie's steady presence and encouragement. Staff members, volunteers, board members, and people from the wider community offered their special remembrances.

We had almost reached the end of the service. It was time for a final prayer of commendation, a last hymn, and a benediction, and Jerry had not spoken. I glanced at him and said, "Are there any others who would like to share with us their memories or thoughts about Eddie?"

No one spoke or moved. I started toward the center of the little altar to offer the closing prayer.

Then, finally, Jerry rose from his seat. I waited. He shook his head as if to clear his mind, and brought his hands to his eyes as if clearing his vision. He gathered focus and spoke.

"Eddie was my friend," he said, "sometimes my only friend. Eddie always had a smile and a hello for me. There were times when I couldn't come in here, times when I couldn't go in anywhere. I didn't have any place to stay. I didn't have any place to eat. But Eddie always made sure when I came to the back door. He couldn't let me in, but he made sure to give me a blanket and a sandwich. I'm alive because Eddie cared. That's all I have to say. And now I want to sing the Bugle Song."

In a clear baritone, he began to sing:

"Day is done
Gone the sun
From the hills
From the lakes
From the sky
Safely rest
All be well
God is nigh."

The words to taps, the day's last call.

The room was quiet. This oft-rejected, broken pilgrim of the streets sat down, and the flute picked up the tune. The melody of re-assurance circled and sounded to us all.

In our hardest moments come the toughest questions. And the deepest answers. No matter what we have been, no matter who we are, no matter how little we have at the end of the day, home and safety are our ultimate destination, healing and wholeness our ultimate abode. Stronger than any illness or evil, able to overcome death itself is the nearness of God, an infinite gentleness able to bear with us our worst, and bring forth in us our fullest and best.

Jerry entered and left the life of the Hoyo community numerous times over the years as he aged. A small circle of care wove itself around him. In his sixties, he was placed in care on a geriatric psychiatry unit, along with others who had had lifelong journeys with mental illness. Among these veterans of the struggle, Jerry was welcomed as a valued comrade. Frail after many years on the street, he transitioned from the hospital to a small nursing home. There he rested, safe and well cared for.

The tenderness of God takes up every moment and aspect of our lives, with care especially to what is most difficult and fearsome and painful. Holding the whole of who we are in an invincible grace, God constantly offers back to us new life, a place in an infinite and abiding circle of care.

3

THE POTTER'S FIELD

Long before I met Sterling, Terri, and Jerry, I had my own experience with mental illness. In the spring of my junior year at Carleton College, I began feeling a nameless sense of worry and anxiety. I had increasing difficulty sleeping. I would lie awake for hours, finally doze off and then awaken again, full of dread, unable to go back to sleep. An unbidden sadness constantly welled up from deep within me. I had trouble concentrating. I couldn't follow the words on a page, and stopped reading and doing class assignments. I began to forget things, and missed appointments and work. I lost my appetite—not just for food, but for day-to-day activity. While walking, I stared down at the ground and shuffled along slowly, the horizon reduced to a circle of a few feet around me. I didn't glance up or look at others. Even simple decisions became wrenchingly difficult. I stopped going to classes and spent several sleepless and tearful nights in the college infirmary.

There were no identifiable external factors to explain the onset of my despair. I had done well in my courses for three years. I was dating a bright, caring woman, and we had spent the spring vacation visiting each other's families. I had recently been elected president of the student body. But now I found myself with no self-confidence, unable to think, and desperate for some kind of help and understanding. Others enjoyed the May sunlight after a long Minnesota winter; I saw only deepening shades of gray.

I dropped out of school and went home to Ann Arbor, Michigan.

There I lay in bed, staring mutely at the ceiling. I didn't eat or talk. The sleepless nights were the worst. I lay in the darkness, certain that I would never be well again. I felt a bump on the back of my head and became convinced that an awful, incurable tumor was slowly killing me.

My parents struggled to understand, and I can only imagine now what it was like for them to see their son in such a state, so far removed from the person they had birthed and raised and loved. They had moved to Ann Arbor the previous fall from Madison, Wisconsin, and didn't know, at first, where to turn, so they called an old family friend back in Madison who was a psychiatrist. He recognized my symptoms as those of a deep depression, but it was 1966 and healing resources were few. Very little was known about the brain, brain cells, and the biochemistry of moods and thought. Two decades would pass before the introduction of the antidepressant Prozac (fluoxetine hydrochloride). Inpatient hospital treatment could last for decades. My parents' friend told them there were two choices: they could admit me to a hospital or simply wait the illness out, hoping that rest, support, and counseling would bring me out of the depths.

On the worst day of my depression, I got out of bed and found the house empty. With no purpose that I can recall, I got into one of our family cars and drove out of town. I entered Interstate 94 and accelerated until I was doing seventy or seventy-five. All I saw was the dark road ahead and, in the distance, three or four thick cement columns in a line, holding up an overpass. As the car approached, the columns grew larger—solid, lifeless stanchions; anonymous gray concrete, the road in shadow underneath. The columns seemed to be inviting me, but I passed through the first series of them and drove on.

My mind registered only the most basic facts. I had no feelings that I can remember, not fear or relief, not sadness or desperation. I wasn't thinking about myself. I had no sense of losing anything, nor any idea about what it might mean to have my life end, no sense of regret or ambivalence. I had no awareness of any possible pain and no thought about how my death might affect my family or friends.

There was no internal dialogue at all. I was not being selfish—I no longer had a sense of self. My universe had shrunk to these few immediate, bare moments with nothing and no one nearby or beyond.

As the next overpass neared, my hands turned toward the columns on the right, held for an instant, and then turned a fraction of an inch or so farther, taking me off the interstate, up the off-ramp and onto a county highway. A mile or so down this road, I turned off to the left on a side road and then onto a narrow dirt track that led to a small clearing in the woods.

I stopped the car at the edge of the clearing and sat with my head down. I was taking shallow breaths. The engine was still running, and my foot was on the clutch. Slowly I turned off the engine, put the gearshift into first, let out the clutch, and peeked out the front window. About twelve feet ahead of me was an ash-filled fire pit. Scattered around the clearing were shards of broken and misfired pottery. A few whole pieces, larger pieces, stood ready for glazing and firing. But no one was around.

For the first time in several months, I experienced a small spark of curiosity. I opened the car door and stepped out. For a moment I stood there, looking over the car door at the pit of ashes and the broken pottery and the formed pieces waiting to be glazed, fired, and brought to life. It mystified me, this place. It seemed an unusual setting—and vulnerable, this clearing where someone had left their life work, their brokenness and unfinished gifts, out in the open and unprotected from whoever might come along.

There was another there with me, unseen: an artist, a potter who plied his craft here, in the middle of nowhere, shaping and reshaping, firing and refiring, making and remaking. In that potter's small field, a feeling of being part, of being connected, of being in touch stirred within me, and I began to wonder: Who is it that works here? When does he or she come? What's this person like who chooses to work outside the walls and create within the natural world?

I took in a few deep breaths and became, for a moment, part of this field of inspiration. Something in me unfroze and warmed at the unexpectedness and grace of this artist's gift. I continued to stand in silence, engaged by a person whose name I knew not, whose face was invisible and yet whose handwork and spirit were so clearly present. Eventually I returned to the car, started the engine up again, backed down the track until I could turn around, and went home.

It is hard to know exactly when, or how, or why healing begins, and for some time, I was still gravely ill. The evening after I returned from the potter's field, I fell to the floor in the family room of our house, crying. Once again, I felt an immeasurable sadness that I was unable to put into words. Once again, my parents were deeply pained at the plight of their son.

The next day, my dad crossed the backyard to the Lutheran church to ask for help from our new pastor, Dick Preis. Dick came over that evening. We sat quietly for a while, and then he suggested that he and I go for a drive. We drove together for perhaps an hour, around the city and out of town for a ways. He seemed to have no destination in mind; there was no hurry to get anyplace. I was not much of a conversationalist: tears and silence, pursed lips and frustrated headshakes were my main means of communication. I was what I was, and Dick accepted that. He didn't ask for more than I could give or be in that moment, didn't try to make me something I was not. He offered the gift of his presence, and in those twilight hours began months of ministry in which we shared the ordinary and daily movements of life. He came to our house. He went with me to visit the doctor. He invited me to ride along as he made calls and went to meetings. He asked me one morning to help mop up the flooded floor of the church basement.

Dick enjoyed the theater, and throughout the summer we went to a number of plays and musicals together. Between the empty world of depression and the intensely distilled, inspired, and cathartic world of the stage, I began to find my way once again in the daily round, the ordinary world of family, friends, and work.

Prior to my illness, Dick and I hardly knew each other; I had not grown up in his church, and we had met only briefly during Christmas vacation a few months before my illness. His style of pastoral care was unorthodox, but remarkably effective. His patience had no limit. He said little, listened deeply even when I had great difficulty articulating what was going on with me. He did not judge. He did not bring false cheer to our meetings. He was a godsend.

Riding with him in his car, or sitting next to him in the theater, I was not defined by my illness; I was more: I was *a person struggling with an illness.* My symptoms alone did not determine me. In relation to Dick, I was a self, a person who experienced in our time together a range of feelings, many and different moments, some extraordinarily difficult and painful, others quite ordinary and commonplace, still others deeply supportive, compassionate, and moving. Over a long summer, as I slowly recovered, Dick gently encouraged me to grow as a person, to stretch into exercise and activities, to share and explore my feelings as they came up, to express my thoughts and hopes, to be honest with others about both my strengths and my vulnerabilities, to find my place in the world. Always, Dick had care for my *soul,* my deepest identity, my wholeness as a person, the source, roots, and ultimate horizon of who I am as a human being. With Dick I experienced a profoundly graceful companionship, a spiritually supportive journey together. Years later, the spirit and art of companioning journey became the heart of a ministry on the streets connecting with, and caring for, others who struggled with mental illness and homelessness.

Through the worst of the illness and on into my summer of recovery, the Spirit was ever at work. I had little awareness of God's presence, especially in my most disturbed and troubled moments. In the depths of the depression, I could not pray or even ask for prayer. I could not read scriptures or even follow a few simple lines on a page. I gazed blankly at a bookmark someone gave me, printed with words from Paul's letter to the Corinthians—"Faith, hope, and love abide, and the greatest of these is love"—but at the time, the words had no meaning. Only the most concrete actions reached me, words made flesh.

When I began to recover and could read again, what spoke to me first was a story from *A Man Called Peter,* Catherine Marshall's biography of her husband, Peter Marshall, an eloquent and powerful preacher. It was not Peter Marshall's sermons, nor his wisdom and success as a pastor, that touched me most; it was an account he gave of walking one foggy night in the countryside, struggling with his own worth and faith. He stopped for some reason, and as the mists swirled about his feet and parted for a moment, he saw that he had come just short of stepping off the edge into a deep abandoned quarry. This barely averted tragedy was a vivid touchstone in Marshall's faith journey. At the edge of the abyss, he experienced a gentle holding, an immediate sense, beyond words, of God's extraordinary care. As much as any scripture or testimony, this moment became a personal parable, a lived story of the Holy present in Peter Marshall's life.

Marshall's story named something that I could only barely sense and feel. The gift of his words encouraged me and rang true. I was no longer at the edge; I had been stopped short of the abyss and began now to patch my life back together. I took a job with the grounds crew at the University of Michigan, laying sod, weeding flower beds, and raking leaves. The sheer physical activity helped. The worst of the depression lifted. The day of the drive down the highway and the experience in the potter's field settled out of consciousness and into the depths of memory, to return to me only after the passage of time.

I went back to college in the fall and took a part in a student production of the musical comedy *Stop the World, I Want to Get Off.* In the middle of rehearsals, I felt myself slipping again. I had to slow down. I dropped out of the production team. My roommate, Joe Spencer, who happened to be the director of the show, understood; he filled in for me until I was ready to rejoin the cast. It was another in a long set of recovery lessons about vulnerability, limits, and our ongoing need for help and support.

As my classmates got on with their lives, planning for graduation and pursuing their goals for work or postgraduate study, I was at a loss. Earlier, I had pictured myself earning a law degree and eventually entering the intense world of politics. That door now appeared to be closing. What I was about to learn was that the experience of mental illness does not necessarily eliminate any particular life activity. It can shake our foundations and call into question our life direction. It can also be a crucible in which we find deep truth about ourselves, and an occasion for distilling new clarity about our purpose and our path. The crisis in my life opened a new door, bearing out a line from Tom Stoppard's play *Rosencrantz and Guildenstern Are Dead*: "Every exit is an entrance somewhere else."

David Maitland, the college chaplain at Carleton, witnessed my struggles. He knew that I had come to school with an interest in religion, and he now suggested that I consider entering a seminary. He didn't know whether it would take me into the ministry, but he encouraged me to enroll for a year to explore where it might lead. "If you decide to continue," he said, "that will be to the good. If you decide to do something else, we will have in the world a layperson with a deeper appreciation of faith and ministry, and that, too, will be good." David had a remarkable optimism, rooted in a sense that always, there is possibility.

Many of us who journey with mental illness have a greater-than-average spiritual sensitivity. That doesn't mean we all find our way into the ministry, but some of us do. For me, the way led to the Chicago Theological Seminary.

During my middler (second) year in seminary, I took a course on the prophet Jeremiah from Joseph Blenkinsopp, a priest who, along with J. R. R. Tolkien and others, had prepared the New Jerusalem translation of the Bible, widely used in the Roman Catholic Church. Jeremiah walks in the marketplace, in the heart of the city, where he is sensitive to the needs of the widows and orphans, the plight of the poor, the cries of the beggars and outcasts. Jeremiah ministers with the sick and the hungry and broken. He calls out to the king and the priestly elite to turn in the direction of compassion and justice. He counsels policies of humility and human care as the first concerns of the nation. Jeremiah speaks in parables; he tells stories and embodies in his own daily life the Holy Spirit, the touch and tenderness of God in the world.

For one class assignment, we were asked to pick a Jeremiah story and discuss the truth it revealed. I chose the story of the prophet's visit to a potter's house, from Jeremiah 18.

Jeremiah watches the potter take a lump of clay, place it on the wheel, and begin to shape it into a simple bowl. The sides gradually rise as the potter's hand shapes the curves and forms the interior with care. Jeremiah watches as the bowl goes off balance and its shape becomes skewed and unworkable. He observes as the potter gradually reworks the clay, fashioning the bowl again, rebuilding the sides once more, and carefully reforming the vessel inside and out. Two times, three, maybe four times or more, the potter shapes and reshapes, works and reworks, this lump of earth.

Jeremiah returns from his visit and uses the image of the potter's hands to help us understand the way of God in the world. God as a gentle potter, One who holds our lives in constant care and persistently shapes and reshapes our journey with us in the direction of well-being—this image of an ever-creative, loving God has remained with me always.

Some folks experience moments of instantaneous illumination—like Saul of Tarsus on the road to Damascus. Truth comes in a flash and with a burning certainty. Not so with me. It took twenty-five years for me to make the connection between my potter's field experience and Jeremiah's, to see the hand of God in those moments of near-suicide, seeking to shape health amid the terrible forces of an illness quickly leading unto death.

My delayed revelation came after I had founded the Mental Health Chaplaincy, and Mary Moeller, a psychiatric nurse educator, came to Seattle to help us with one of our first conferences on the theme of "Soul, Psychiatry, and Society." Mary showed slides of people's brains, those of individuals in states of health and those in the midst of depression, bipolar disorder, and schizophrenia. The images showed the chemical activity in various areas of the brain. The brain of a person in the midst of the grandiosity, euphoria, and elation of mania fairly glowed with bright oranges, reds, and yellows—the energy of a brain swung into the highest mood extremes. The brain of a person hearing hallucinatory voices showed activity in the brain centers that process sound, despite the absence of an auditory stimulus.

Mary showed the brain of a person recovered from depression. There was a healthy richness of energy—feelings being processed, senses reporting, ideas online, memory active, and imagination at work; it was perfectly clear that there were multiple centers and levels of life and activity, but nowhere near the blazing brain of bipolar disorder. Mary then showed that same person's brain in the midst of depression. Much of the color, the energy, the activity was absent. Large areas of the brain lay dormant or nearly so. Those areas that functioned gave off only small amounts of energy, showing up in fragments and patches of blue, dark green, occasionally small areas of pale aqua or violet—signs of little cell activity, little biochemical process or connections.

Tears filled my eyes. That had been *my* brain! No wonder I had felt so leaden; no wonder my sense of being almost paralyzed. My brain had shut down to such an extent that I could only shuffle along or lie flat on my bed. No wonder I didn't talk. Thoughts and ideas, if they came at all, got stuck and didn't trigger the connections that would allow me to open my mouth, form words, or respond to others. No wonder I saw nothing beyond a few feet away from me; no wonder I didn't lift my head. And now I realized that the centers of visual consciousness in my brain were not producing any kind of realistic picture of the world. No wonder I felt helpless and hopeless—my brain was accurately communicating a state of imbalance, disconnection, and malfunction. I had little to no higher functioning of mind; no access to memory, imagination, or alternatives.

Ordinary drawings of the brain make it look like a kind of soft, rubbery mass. I have a model brain that I use in lectures. It looks pretty solid but comes neatly apart for demonstration of what is inside. I can lift off the frontal lobe, where neuroscientists suggest that significant areas of thought, imagination, and inspiration are centered. I can pull off a second, deeper section that includes multiple areas where important activities relating to sensation, emotion, mood, memory, and motivation are found. I can hold in my hand the brain stem, where basic information about the environment is processed and reactions immediately organized. The model suggests that the brain is a solid piece of hardware, a collection of neatly fitting parts and readily traceable connecting wires linking everything together.

But the brain is not a computer. Each of the billions of cells floating in the brain's common sea is particular and distinct from its neighbor cells. Every neuron is a kind of microscopic island. At one end of the neuron are up to ten thousand arms, each tipped with an intricately operating port that receives messages arriving via biochemical boats across the cranial ocean from surrounding island cells. Cells are not plugged into each other, but signal one another from a distance, transmitting information, encouragement, and warning. One cell communicates to another by activating molecules docked or at the ready, able to take up an impulse of information and ferry its value and vitality to the appropriate receptor sites on the arms or dendrites of nearby cells. At each of these receptor sites, new molecules are waiting to be energized and fired off to carry the incoming messages to the cell nucleus or center. One cell alone may be receiving the cargo of hundreds of messaging ships, arriving at several thousands of ports.

In a well-functioning brain, these varied energies are constantly flowing. As they reach a cell, they are channeled together from the many receptor sites into the cell nucleus. The pulsing river of information coming into the cell center is further processed by a multitude of up to one hundred thousand protein molecules. Each of these minute agents can "view" the constantly arriving data from at least three different angles and make its unique contribution to the emerging consensus about what this cell will send on to its neighbors. Thus every neuron in the brain is, to some degree, its own tiny center of interpretation and decision.

We are only beginning to understand the nature of the sea between the cells in the brain and the way the diverse ferrying systems are activated by one cell and offloaded at the receptor sites of neighboring cells. Medications treating mental illness are thought to work at least in part at these port sites of the synapses and in the synapse itself, the ocean of space between cells.

Adding richness to the process of interpretation and decision in the cell nucleus are additional flows of information arriving through the walls of the cell nucleus itself. It turns out that the wall of each neuron nucleus is not the smooth, watertight container we might imagine, but a semipermeable membrane, an intricate globe of pumps, another system of gateways leading into and out of the cell. Through this wall passes another whole set of important data, elements of sensation, emotion, and ideation, flows of stress and emphasis that modulate or amplify the decisions being processed in the cell center. We are just beginning to explore how our moods, thoughts, and experience of the world are organized and influenced by this system of cellular interactions.

There is yet a third kind of process operating in and upon the cells of our brains. The activity of each cell, the clustering and connecting of cells into complex areas of human capacity and experience—the work of our body as a whole—generates power and fields of energy. Danah Zohar, author of *The Quantum Self,* suggests that these waves of energy play into one another and finally harmonize from moment to moment within each neuron or across a complex society of cells, contributing a final degree of unity to our experience at every level of our lives. Dr. Zohar sees these moments of harmony as actual expressions of spiritual activity.

From Christian tradition comes the beautiful image that God's eye is on even the tiniest sparrow, and the wonderful thought that God numbers the hairs upon our head. These images suggest God's intimate care for, and involvement in, the smallest moments of our existence. Consider that the Spirit of God, the intentional, creative, healing, loving, and life-redeeming power of God, is active on every level down to, and tenderly including, each cell of our brains. Consider that the Spirit of God, the gentle energy of God, is active in the molecular, atomic, and subatomic shaping of the synapses between brain cells, and attends to every movement across these infinitesimal spaces. Consider that the Spirit of God is active in the construction of each intricate cell wall, and in the flow that they allow. Consider that the Spirit of God is constantly active in the process by which each cell receives, interprets, and contributes its part to the ever-unfolding whole of our experience.

Consider, if you will, that the brain is not simply a physical organ, but the richest locus of spiritual presence within us.

Consider that the activity of the Spirit at this cellular level of our existence is not in any way imperious, dogmatic, or domineering, but extraordinarily gentle, a deeply loving presence that gives counsel and comfort freely, seeks our well-being, promotes our healing, honors our worth, and celebrates our sacredness.

At that moment on Interstate 94, that instant in which the steering wheel turned and suicide was averted, much in my brain was shut down by the forces of depression. The memory of better times was inactive, unavailable; my ability to imagine possibilities and envision alternatives, blank. At that moment, thought had stopped and my emotions had emptied to the point of utter detachment. The brain that had served me so well for twenty-one years was barely conscious. My life was about to end, and the reality of death was nothing more than a mindless absence.

What would an image of my brain have shown in that last moment? I think of the tiny patches of color in Mary Moeller's slide of the depressed brain. Which cells had remained active, or barely so, in my own brain at that dark time?

Something had been desperately amiss within my brain, and yet God still held me in relationship. The Spirit of God served to keep and embrace me. Those cells that no longer functioned, the misbegotten molecules, the scattered and silent atoms—God still valued all that had made me and held the whole of my life, present, past, and future, in an infinite love. So it is whenever any one of us is in such a crisis: the Spirit of God steadfastly nurtures every possibility within us for life. God is ever supportive of the best outcome at every point and port of potential within us.

The dynamics of illness are real. The weight of disorder is undeniable. None of us comes into the world with infinite supplies of positive energy; all of us are finite and mortal. Our bodies and brains are vulnerable to disease and disorder, and in the end, death. We are mistaken if we believe that our lives maintain themselves—that *we alone* keep ourselves going. It is only within a rich and supportive environment, composed of our relationships with others and with God, that life is possible.

By employing the capacities of reason and the skills of research, science and medicine can teach us about the patterns and processes of our existence. But to speak of the whole of our lives and the deep, particular truths that we each embody, we must draw upon the wisdom of faith, the language and art of the Spirit, and our experience as souls. Dr. David Avery, a friend and colleague of mine, has thought upon these things, both as a man of faith and as a psychiatrist and researcher. Science, he suggests, speaks in theory about what is true in general, constantly testing beliefs, understandings, predictions, and practices through careful controlled experiments. Spiritual conversation focuses ultimately on what is unique and particular, irreducible and immeasurable, in our experience. We can explore our faith, question and sharpen our beliefs, test our religious and spiritual practices, and give witness to the presence of the Holy in our lives, but we cannot scientifically prove our claims concerning God.

When I contemplate my near-suicide, it is a matter of faith for me to say that, in that crucial moment years ago, God was at work in the potter's field. Jeremiah had seen in the patient, careful, clay-stained hands of an ancient craftsman outward and visible signs of One who is invisible and tenderly at work within us all. In the immediate moment of my experience, I saw no potter; I saw fragments of evidence and felt a lingering presence. I felt the energy of an artist worked deeply into the art and stored, ready for release.

It has taken me decades to reflect on this painful, but generative, spiritual moment in my life and find in that event the movement of the Spirit. I knew the Jeremiah story all along, but I did not know the complex clay of my own being and bodiedness; I had little appreciation for how the Spirit proceeds in our lives to share in, and help shape, who we are.

For more than forty years now, I have been on a pilgrimage, seeking the way of God in the world. Looking back through all I have experienced and learned, in company with my brothers and sisters on the street and with colleagues in hospitals and clinics, I have come to this: At the most intimate levels of my being and becoming, in the particular moments of deepest depression, God was far from absent. The love of God, the life of God, the Spirit of God was active, holding every dormant and disabled cell, cradling with compassion the deadened networks and disordered processes of my depressed and suicidal brain. The Spirit battled for life in every possible synapse, and for the potential health of every available cell.

The complexity of even one moment, one slight turn of the wheel, is ultimately beyond our imagination. Perhaps in my case the Spirit affected one sufficient atom, or one necessary molecule, of one neurotransmitter at one port site of one cell, enough to tip the balance toward renewed life in this world. For me, at a crucial juncture, the weight of depression lifted sufficiently for life to continue, allowing time for new supports and services to arrive in aid of the Spirit's care.

The Spirit invites a partnership in the healing process, a partnership that, on the human side, involves medicine, counseling, and companionship. Such a partnership of the Holy and the human helped me, over the course of time, to live with my vulnerability to depression. As I consider the wide range of people who suffer from depression and other forms of mental illness, though, I find no formula that enables me to define a specific balance between the role of the Spirit and the human practices of care. In many cases, the immediate and intensive help of others is necessary, giving the Spirit time to bring forth the fullness of healing.

The Spirit is God's tender gift, working with us without regard to merit and with respect for each individual's unique circumstances. The Spirit of God—the same Spirit that was, and is, at the heart of Creation, the "divine wind sweeping over the waters" at the beginning of time (Gen. 1:2); the "Holy Spirit" that filled Jesus as he began his ministry (Luke 4:1, 18); the Spirit whose fruit is "love, joy, peace, patience, kindness, goodness, trustfulness, gentleness and self-control" (Gal. 5:22); the "Holy Spirit who dwells in us" (2 Tim. 1:14)—has been equally engaged with Sterling, Terri, Jerry, you, and me. In the hands of God every one of us is infinitely worthy; in the mind and heart of God, each of us is of eternal value. And no matter what the odds, no matter what influence, illness, or evil threatens, God struggles for our healing and salvation.

PART II

The Life of the Soul

The love of God, active in the Spirit, moves in the world to shape and care for our souls—our deepest identity as persons and our wholeness as human beings. The Spirit of God approaches us each with infinite tenderness, honors us in our freedom, treats us with dignity, and becomes a part of us on our journey. The Spirit embraces our lives as sacred and, working with us, weaves the many threads of our existence into an ever-growing fullness. In this process our souls emerge over time, in our earthly lives and beyond.

The Spirit works in company with others in our lives. To be human is not simply to find a life alone with God, but to be born in relationship with others. When we are well, we rejoice in the company of those we love. When we are at our most vulnerable, when we are ill, we especially need the presence and support of family, neighbors, friends, and caregivers. The soul thrives not in isolation, but in community.

Long ago, I thought of the soul as some "thing" within me, a kind of golden walnut located near my heart. I believed that my soul might be damaged by illness or bad behavior and that, at the time of my death, I would be saved only if I had said the right things, believed hard enough, or trusted sufficiently. I had the notion that my eternal standing was in some grave doubt, that the thread of connection

45

between God and my soul could be easily snapped; that God could simply choose to drop me and my soul into the fires of hell for an ever-punishing and unending refinement.

In the midst of my suicidal depression, I experienced a kind of living hell. It was not fiery, however; it was cold and barren, a plunge through absolute isolation toward a numb and obliterating death. My soul seemed to have withered and disappeared to nothing.

In the course of healing and recovery, in the company of the Spirit, in being companioned by others and in companioning sisters and brothers on their journeys from the street to stability, I have come to a different understanding of the human soul. Our souls are our deepest and fullest identity, our wholeness in relation to others and to God. Our souls, no matter how disturbed from forces within, or battered by the world, are constantly held in care. I have come to understand that God's Spirit of love is ever active, never withdrawn from us.

Companionship gives human form to the movement of the Spirit, shaping personal relationships that support healing and nurture our souls. The stories in Part II illustrate the way of companionship, a spiritual journey that leads from suffering and estrangement through an ever-present grace to new life.

4

APPROACHING MARY

Fourth and Pike form a busy intersection in downtown Seattle. Traffic rushes by, and pedestrians hurry along the sidewalk to get to work or shop or take refuge from the chill in a Starbucks café. On the southwest corner is a Rite Aid drugstore, and in front of it, across the sidewalk, is where I first saw Mary, huddled back against a large blue mailbox at the curb and surrounded by two black plastic trash bags with yellow drawstrings and an old, dirty white laundry bag. Mary's little fortification protected her from anyone who might try to come too near.

Mary stood not much taller than her bags. She was wearing several coats, in layers, and a scarf around her face. Her droopy hat shielded her from the winter rain: the same hat that she wore through the spring winds and under the summer sun. If people approached her, she turned away. Now and then a Good Samaritan offered her food or money or tried to engage her in conversation, but she always turned away.

As I watched her that first time, she did this again and again. Finally, at some unseen prompting, she methodically gathered up her three bags. She waited until no one else stood at the crosswalk, then shuffled to the curb and, when the light changed and the cars running east stopped, crossed Pike Street to the opposite corner. There she set up her fortress again, this time with a row of newspaper vending machines at her back. She stayed there for another half hour, hunkered down in her little redoubt, always turning away if anyone came near. All I knew of Mary were these small maneuvers that kept the world at a distance, and I wondered how to reach her.

I had noticed that, when Mary was in the crosswalk, she plunged straight ahead and did not turn away from people walking toward her. The crosswalk, three-plus feet between those parallel lines, apparently offered some safety; in this narrow zone, a braver, more confident and purposeful Mary moved forth.

I waited from across Fourth Avenue until Mary gathered her bundles and prepared to cross now in my direction. She started out, and so did I. In the middle of the intersection we passed, and for the briefest of moments we were face to face, although Mary's head was down and I could see only the crown and brim of her hat. She trudged on, and at the corner where I had been standing she once more set up her fortification, this time with a big concrete waste-bin holder at her back.

For several weeks Mary and I passed in the crosswalks around Fourth and Pike. Once she lifted her head and our eyes met for less than a second. A few days later our eyes met again, long enough for me to smile and nod. After a third or fourth such moment over the next few days, Mary nodded toward me, ever so slightly—or perhaps I just wished it to be so. She seemed to recognize me, although I had the feeling that, in her mind, I was at best some distant relative.

Several months of these momentary crosswalk meetings went by. I would say hello, and Mary would respond with a fleeting look of recognition and, again, the tiniest nod of her head. I slowed as we met—not so as to linger, but to give us at least one more second of presence with each other. I did that also as I passed by her fortresses on the sidewalk. At the end of one day, as she set off for wherever she hid away at night, I offered to help her carry a bag. She smiled but said no and kept on moving. We had had our first conversation, brief but pleasant. We had become not just two human beings passing on the street, but rudimentary neighbors.

One summer afternoon I found Mary sitting on her laundry bag and reading from a book in her hand: a soft, worn black cover; gilt-edged pages; and ribbons to mark a couple favorite passages—a well-used personal Bible. I stopped a few yards off.

I smiled and said, "A good book."

She glanced up and said, "Yes." Then she turned her head down again.

"It's a book I use a lot, too," I said.

She looked up once more and nodded.

We had now had two conversations.

Approaching Mary was a learning experience for me. It was tempting to be more assertive, to move in closer as soon as she showed the slightest sign of an invitation, but something urged me to restraint. The street was Mary's home. I had happened to find her that day out on her porch, as it were. I was a neighbor passing by, not a guest arriving for a visit. It would take months for us to establish a relationship of trust and confidence.

I began stopping more frequently, and as our conversations grew longer, I learned more about Mary. She was in her forties and had no family in the area. She had come to Seattle years ago with a friend and found employment as a housekeeper in hotels and private homes. She was proud of her work. Her native language was Spanish. And she had a dream: she wanted a room or a small apartment, and in exchange she would do some cleaning in her building for others. It seemed reasonable to her. She would give service; she would be given housing in a safe setting. She couldn't articulate this desire much further.

Mary's elemental wariness went beyond protecting herself from tangible threats. Occasionally she would glance around and put her finger to her lips, as if to say, "We are being watched; someone is listening." Her hopes and dreams were constantly vitiated by this vague, persistent fearfulness, a force that could not be spoken of. It was as if she lived in children's books where monsters hide under the bed, shadows take frightening shapes, and invisible creatures threaten. This was the world of Mary's illness self, created not by dreams or literary inspiration, but by the disorder in her brain. She could not simply wake up and end the chapter; she couldn't put the book down and take up her usual life again. She wouldn't even consider going to a shelter.

As it happened, I knew of a "safe haven" apartment building being opened by the Downtown Emergency Service Center, a local agency serving the most vulnerable among Seattle's homeless individuals. It was a pilot project, funded by the federal government, designed so that outreach workers could bring people directly off the street and provide them with a room of their own, without eligibility requirements or other barriers. I showed her a brochure created by a design student, with pictures of the building: a view of the entrance, a typical room furnished with a single bed, a simple table, and space to store what was important or valuable to the person.

"Mary," I said, "you can live here. You can help in the common room, maybe help other residents. There is a room for you if you want."

Mary glanced through the photos and showed some interest, but she was ambivalent. Her illness self was dominant; her fear and confusion kept her just beyond touch with reality. Yet her familiar self— her healthy self, her self that existed before her illness—was there, too. Our relationship, now cultivated over many months, had nurtured the hidden, healthy side of her and made it available in her— not at all times, and not yet as strongly as the force of her illness self, but occasionally and in some discernible degree.

By now, Mary trusted me enough to let me introduce her to an outreach worker connected with the safe haven. He was an extraordinarily gentle and compassionate man, a compadre who could speak fluent Spanish with Mary—an important gift. He encouraged her, explained to her how easily she could make the change. It was a beautiful day when Mary agreed to go take a look at the room that was waiting for her, and a special day indeed when she agreed to move in.

I visited her a week later. The sun beamed through the window and shone on her table, where her comfortable old black Bible with the gilt-edged pages lay open. Just moving off the street into housing is healing in itself, and Mary looked better already, less frail and more relaxed. I sat down and we talked. I asked her what she had been reading in the Good Book.

She pointed to the page on the table between us, verses 2–10 from Psalm 139:

Thou knowest when I sit down and when I rise up:
thou discernest my thoughts from afar.
Thou searchest out my path and my lying down,
    and are acquainted with all my ways.

. . . .

Thou dost beset me behind and before,
    and layest thy hand upon me . . .

Whither shall I go from thy Spirit?
    Or whither shall I flee from thy presence?
If I ascend to heaven, thou art there!
    If I make my bed in Sheol, thou art there!
If I take the wings of the morning
    and dwell in the uttermost parts of the sea,
even there thy hand shall lead me,
    and thy right hand shall hold me.

The verses, together with Mary's story, reminded me of a Hasidic tale. A little boy sits on his grandfather's lap. Grandfather says, "I will give you a groschen if you can tell me where God is." The little boy looks up at his grandfather and says, "I will give you two groschen if you can tell me where God isn't."

As the Psalmist so beautifully put it, God is present in our every moment. So it was with Mary. Even as she was driven to the margins of our community, even as she grew more and more distant, alienated, and fearful of everyone; even as her state of disorientation and terror created a huge chasm between herself and those who might have helped her, God was with her.

What had affected me initially was the evidence of Mary's illness:

her protectiveness, the layers of clothing, the bags and bundles she carried, the weary and fearful look in her eyes, her silence. For me, these were outward and visible signs of an illness identity, a frightened, burdened, struggling Mary, but also a Mary who was a survivor.

Mary lived on the margins, but in some essential ways she was like all of us. We are never simply one self, never a single and constant pattern of self. Our personhood is complex. We have within us numerous identities, multiple patterns and dimensions of ourselves. I, for example, am a son, a husband, a father, a minister, and a citizen. I am also a man in perpetual recovery from mental illness, a man whose illness self occasionally pushes its way to the surface and, for a while, takes over. We all have our vulnerabilities, whether they be illnesses or disabilities physical or mental, lack of self-confidence, uncertainty about the future, loneliness, or any of a hundred other conditions. In bed with the flu or a back injury, we may be unable to focus on much of anything but our condition. When we are out of work and worried about making the rent or the next mortgage payment, or paying for food or bills piling up, it's easy to let our troubles, which are real and urgent, govern our moods and our behavior. Our familiar self—the self that is loving, kind, generous, and caring—can become submerged, as despair, pain, or anxiety dominates our life. Someone meeting us for the first time in such circumstances might think that this is how we are and have always been. We know, however, that they are wrong; this self, worried or preoccupied or wracked with pain, cannot and does not define us absolutely.

So, too, with Mary. What I saw at first was only one side of her: her street self, her illness self. But even in those earliest moments of our relationship, more of Mary was available: the ability to make a number of decisions, the strength to move and to carry her bags, a level of intention, a hidden history, a journey, a today, a tonight, and a tomorrow. Slowly over time and in our many brief moments together, Mary's fuller and more familiar self emerged—the woman behind the illness and homelessness, the person whom friends and family used to know. In a fleeting smile, in a momentary flash of openness and trust, in a tentative hello, I began to see Mary, the multidimensional person.

And particularly in that moment when I encountered Mary sitting on her laundry bag with her Bible in her hand, I had a glimpse of her spiritual identity, a glimpse of her soul. It was only a hint, but it had to do with nothing less than her wholeness as a person, the fullness of her selfhood in relation to God.

Mary's story bears out the Psalmist's poetic reflections on the omnipresence of God. The Spirit of God is active in all of the occasions that constitute our life. The work of the Spirit gives rise to faith in all its many forms—physical, sensual, emotional, intellectual, personal, social, and mystical. The act of birth is a moment of faith, the promise of the Spirit emergent in the world. The touch and sounds and fragrances, the warm, sweet milk and looks of love nurturing us as infants, are continuing expressions of faith, a reservoir of sacraments that give encouragement to our souls.

Faith begs to be understood as something actively expressed and experienced in the context of human relationships. Every small mercy or ministration that soothes and delights us—a gift of flowers in the hospital, a pat on the back or a high five for a job well done—is a moment of foundational faith, imbuing our souls with divine feeling. In the patterns of care and deeds of kindness, the structures of our belief and understanding are formed, and our ideas of self and world come to consciousness. With each intimate act of love and sympathy, empathy and compassion, respect and honor, our faith deepens and our souls grow in relation to one another. As we share in play and school and work, and the life of family and neighborhood, community, country, and world, we experience the movement of the Spirit; our faith expands and our souls develop into ever-larger realms of meaning and purpose.

This is the life of the soul, our spiritual identity, which nothing —neither illness, nor disorders of the brain, nor death itself—can destroy.

Mary is a soul, a wholeness that includes the realities of her illness and homelessness, her healing and recovery, her history, her fullness and ever-emerging completeness as a person. Sterling is a soul, Terri is a soul, Jerry is a soul. Each, like you and me, is a wholeness, a healing, a shaping and reshaping, ever in process.

The life of the soul is rooted in faith, in the presence of God and the touch of the Spirit in every moment of our becoming. No matter how powerful other forces are in our lives, the love of God holds and keeps us each. God's unceasing love for us and care for our souls is a gift, a grace available in every moment.

Once while watching a film on Buddhism, I was struck by the daily practice of a monk in a rural monastery. Each morning he went to a small clearing in the woods and walked a path of seven flat stones. In the early years he walked the path back and forth quickly, many times a day. Over the decades, he had slowed down, sometimes taking a whole day to walk the seven stones just once. By the time the film was shot, the monk, now very old, spent his whole day taking but one step. His goal, he said, was to experience all that there was to know of the Holy in that one step. He stood for hours at the beginning of the path, and raised his foot as slowly and carefully as possible, and held it as long as he was able in the air, and then as slowly and carefully as possible set his foot down on the first stone and there left it to sense and feel and contemplate and become and share and enter into the mystery of that one step in the world.

Jesus walked for three years within a territory we would consider small, and he was never in a hurry. It was not his purpose to build great highways and magnificent edifices, or a vast movement or organization. He stopped constantly wherever his way took him, to be with whomever he found by the side of the road. He stopped especially for those who hurt most, and were most despised and rejected. He joined in their paralysis and pain, identified with their loneliness and isolation. Wherever he went, and with whomever he paused, Jesus witnessed to the healing and whole-making love of God constantly at work in every soul. In story after story after story in the

Gospels, we see his steps slowed down to translucent moments of faith, moments in which the healing, life-giving grace of the Spirit is deeply and surely revealed.

I was called to the hospital on a Sunday evening about a woman, Sylvie, who came to the emergency room weeping and in despair. Some weeks before, she had been admitted to the psychiatric unit in an episode of mania, and staff were concerned now that she was plunging into the depths of depression. But she had been taking her medication. Her mood had been stable and her recovery going well—until that morning in church.

Sylvie, a woman in her thirties, tall and athletic, sat on a gurney covered by a white sheet, and I sat on a plastic chair off to one side. She remembered me from visits on the ward. I told her I just wanted to be there, to listen.

Sylvie, her lips pulled tight, continued crying quietly, and I handed her a Kleenex. In time, I asked her gently if she could help me understand what was happening.

"I went to church this morning," she said.

I nodded.

"They shunned me."

I opened my eyes wider and tilted my head in some astonishment. I knew about shunning as a spiritual practice, but it is rare and I'd never heard of a specific instance.

"They told me to go away. They told the people to ignore me. My family, too." She paused for a moment and breathed rapidly as if readying for a struggle. "Because of how I was at church before. When I was manic—my standing up and all my talking and what I did when I was ill. That's all I've ever heard. How evil we all are and how God will punish us."

She opened her hands in front of her, as if to push back at the people in the church, the pastor, me, God, anybody who once more tried to control or crush her soul.

"Sylvie, you are not bad," I said.

Sylvie pounded her fist on the gurney distractedly. "They don't understand. I was sick." She paused again, glanced at me. "And now I'm getting better and they condemn me."

Sylvie had turned to her church for comfort, and what she got instead was a diagnosis of unredeemable guilt and a heaping dose of judgment. I said I would be glad to meet with her and talk more about the issues with the church and her faith journey. I assured her she did not have to endure this alone.

Sylvie was not readmitted to the hospital that night. She called a friend who was not a member of her church; the friend picked her up and spent the night with her. The next day, Sylvie met with her mental health counselor and her doctor for follow-up care. Later in the afternoon I met with her again, this time in my office, an informal space in a multipurpose room with some comfortable chairs and a sofa. Sylvie came in, more relaxed than the day before and eager to tell me about her past and the details of her recent illness experience.

Sylvie described the God of her religion as a figure of anger and judgment who granted salvation to only a handful of the most faithful and pure. All her life she tried to live in a godly way, and she had been an exemplary church member until the onset of her illness. When that happened, she went to church and prayed fervently and loudly. She took to wearing a strange costume and proclaimed the beginning of a new holy order. She lit what she called eternal candles and tried to keep them burning perpetually throughout the sanctuary. She announced to all that she was the "thirty-third-year messenger of God."

In her illness, fragments of religious practice and thought were patched together into a highly personal set of beliefs and behaviors. Her brain in its illness borrowed bits and pieces of common spiritual language and symbolism, such as Jesus's age at his Crucifixion (thirty-three) and the notion of an eternal flame, and formed from them this extraordinary array of symptoms. Sylvie's actions arose from the disturbance in her broken brain.

With treatment and care in the hospital, Sylvie's symptoms disappeared. It was then that she had returned to church, hoping to find a place of support for her healing, but instead she found rejection. The ushers immediately called one of the pastors, who escorted her to the door and informed her that she was being shunned. He told her she was banned from the church. Her congregation was implementing a centuries-old practice rooted in a specific interpretation of a biblical precedent. For Sylvie, obviously, it was devastating.

Sylvie spoke at some length about her religious history, and eventually I asked if she would share with me her earliest memory of the Holy: When in her life had she first become aware of the sacred or experienced the presence of God?

There was a long silence as she thought back through her young adulthood and school-age years. Finally she smiled.

"I was five," she said. "It was summer, and the sun was beginning to set. I was sitting in our front yard under a weeping willow tree, with branches hanging down around me, like a gauzy curtain. A soft breeze began to blow. The leaves touched me gently, and I knew that God was with me."

Sylvie stopped, and her face lit up. "God doesn't hate me," she said.

"That's right," I said. "So this is where we will begin the journey now, from under that willow tree. The church may have left you. God never has."

Thus began several months of soul care together. Sylvie and I established a basic reference point, a root faith experience of God's presence and touch in her life. We sorted through the symptoms she had experienced, recognizing them not as revelations flowing from the Spirit, but as signs of a brain disorder that borrowed and distorted the trappings of religious tradition. Sylvie came to understand that her behavior in church, her grandiose statement that she was the thirty-third-year messenger, her bizarre costume and insistence on an eternal candle-lighting ritual—these were fueled by her bipolar disorder.

Sylvie's illness identity had overwhelmed her familiar self. Her strange behavior masked her core spiritual identity. People in her church couldn't help believing she had gone astray and perhaps even become, in an ancient phrase common in scriptural terminology, possessed by demons. Even Sylvie felt, she said, as if her soul was lost.

But Sylvie was not evil. Her brain chemistry was unbalanced. Her soul was not lost; it was doing battle with a medical condition that had warped her sense of the Holy.

The Spirit of God in the world inspires moments of faith. Moments of faith, emerging and developing one into the next and flourishing over time in each person, give rise to the framework and fullness of the soul. Human souls called together by the Spirit form spiritual communities to share their experiences of the Holy. They become congregations and take shape in history as religions: peoples bound together in institutions embodying their basic beliefs, scripture, theology, the rituals and practices of worship, service, and action.

Religions have their own impact on the soul. At its best, religious life provides care for the soul and invites all into fellowship, including especially the lost and the least, the most wounded and vulnerable. Religious tradition helps us discern what is truly of God, as opposed to what is of illness and disorder. Religion at its best is an ever-growing repository of wisdom and learning, able to assist souls with understanding and compassion in the struggle with illness, including illnesses rooted in a brokenness of the brain. Religion at its best provides a wealth of resources to amplify the healing that comes from the hand of the physician and pharmacist. Clergy and congregations have the capacity to aid the redemptive work of the Spirit in the face of mental illness. At their best, communities of faith provide a haven within which we can share our unique personal stories and locate ourselves within a larger horizon of meaning. It was right for Sylvie to go to her church to seek help in making sense of her journey at a difficult juncture.

Unfortunately, however, relatively few clergy and congregations are equipped to care for souls struggling with mental illness. Symptoms of neurobiological disorder can be diagnosed as sin. Some churches do, indeed, shun the sick. Others simply neglect to care. Still others prescribe routines of prayer or penance, blaming the parishioner's lack of faith if the illness persists. Pastors who will gladly go to the bedside of the cancer patient or the heart attack victim, or visit regularly in the nursing home, all too rarely visit the psychiatric unit or call on a church member living in a group home run by a community mental health program.

Our religious traditions have little to say about the experience of mental illness. There are too few stories to help us frame the illness journey in faith terms, and precious few places in our congregations where souls may gather with one another for spiritual support. Sylvie is far from alone in seeking the solace of spiritual community and coming away with ashes, marked as unacceptable, unclean, or unwanted.

As Sylvie and I continued to meet, we worked on her concern about the quasi-religious quality of her symptoms and how real they seemed to her at the time. She was full of questions: Why did her illness express itself in religious terms? Where did the idea that she was the thirty-third-year messenger come from? Why the strange clothing and the candles?

Sylvie's manic behavior fit a recognizable pattern. Once I worked with a woman who walked around wrapped in a white sheet and carrying a huge scrapbook. She told everyone she was the Prophet Christa, and her book contained a special plan to make peace in the Middle East. During the time of the first Gulf War, I worked with Darnell, who marched for days along the waterfront, believing that President Bush had appointed him to patrol the Port of Seattle and watch out for an invasion by sea. As part of his duties, he spent hours each morning polishing a drinking fountain with a toothbrush to get it ready for inspection. And then there was Sandra. Sandra, who lived in a local park, could go on for hours about how she was the wife of the former Beatles drummer Ringo Starr and was composing a rock opera that would bring together the Rolling Stones and the Beatles for the performance.

Such grandiosely expansive notions are common to persons in the manic phase of bipolar disorder. In the midst of a manic episode, the brain, in its complexity, can draw on the wide range of data and images available from life experience and popular culture. Sylvie's symptoms took a quasi-religious form, as did the symptoms of the "Prophet Christa." Darnell's symptoms took a quasi-military form. Sandra's symptoms took form in terms of the pop music industry, and her elevated mood led her to the extravagant fantasy of being in partnership with celebrities.

Sylvie's illness manifested in symptoms with an extraordinary and specific quasi-spiritual content that seemed very real to her and extremely worrisome and frightening to those around her. Both she and the congregation treated her words and behavior exclusively in religious terms, with no thought that this was an illness experience caused by a broken or malfunctioning brain. It wasn't easy coming to a fuller understanding of Sylvie's condition and situation.

In caring for the soul of anyone who is in struggle with a brain disorder, it is essential to clarify what is of the illness and what is of the Spirit. The roots of faith and the life of the soul are in the gifts of the Spirit. The symptoms of a mental disorder are the result of a malfunctioning in the brain.

When the biochemistry of the brain is unbalanced, when the cells are not connecting effectively with each other, when the brain is disturbed, the symptoms that emerge follow certain general patterns. The content, however, will be particular and unique to each person. Grandiosity is a symptom of mania, the "up" pole of bipolar disorder, but the way grandiosity is expressed will vary from person to person; it may present itself in Sandra's high-flying entertainment venture, or it may be expressed in more pedestrian ways such as bursts of anger, irritation, or enthusiasm out of proportion to the circumstances.

Each type of illness expresses itself according to its own patterns. Hallucinations and delusions, for example, are generally symptoms of schizophrenia—as when a woman I'll call Veronica believed she saw a store-window mannequin come alive and start talking to her, or when Al heard God's voice in the shower telling him to stop wasting water because he was hopelessly dirty and there was no way he would ever be clean. Both were in fact experiencing schizophrenic episodes.

One frequent symptom of depression is an overwhelming sense of guilt. During a single week in the hospital, I visited with three different patients who were convinced they had committed the "unpardonable sin." Dee, in her depression, had stopped going to her Bible study group. David, a mild-mannered man who volunteered in a mission soup kitchen, swore and used God's name in vain while working on the serving line when some hot chili spilled on the floor. Elliot stopped paying his bills, including his pledge to his church. Each person believed that these actions constituted sins for which there could be no forgiveness.

God was not speaking to Al in the shower; his neurotransmitters were creating hallucinations and playing havoc with his sense of reality. Missing Bible study, swearing, and defaulting on your church pledge are not gross religious felonies that warrant eternal damnation. When such commonplace occurrences become coupled with overwhelming despair, hopelessness, and guilt, it is a signal that something has gone awry in the parts of the brain that regulate feelings and emotions.

In recovery from their illnesses, Sylvie, Sandra, Veronica, Dee, David, Elliot, and Al discovered that they were not alone. They came to understand that a brain malfunction is a sickness, not a sin. Just as dreams are scenarios created by our brains during sleep, when much of our thinking capacity is offline, hallucinations, delusions, mania, and suicidal ideation are extraordinary states of being that originate in the brain—and not a sign of God's harsh judgment. Dreams and brain disorders alike are a reminder of our complexity as humans, a reminder that our brains produce more than rational activity and conscious awareness. Our minds are always larger than we know.

As I worked with Sylvie, I encouraged her to continue meeting with her doctor and nurse, stick with her treatment, and take care of herself physically as well. This is essential advice for all who are in recovery. Just as a broken leg does not mend itself overnight, the brain takes time to become restored once more to its fullest functioning.

One time when we met, Sylvie brought a cherry pie, a pint of ice cream, and two cartons of milk. She had been thinking about her grandmother, who had taught her how to bake pies. Her grandmother had also taught her songs that the two of them sang together.

"My grandma," Sylvie said, "believed that the soul is made up of many songs." She began singing in a warm, rich voice:

"'Tis a gift to be simple
'Tis a gift to be free
'Tis a gift to come down
Where we ought to be . . ."

The soul is indeed made of many songs. As Sylvie and I met over time, she shared the songs of her life and the many moments of faith that nourished her soul. She explored new religious resources and practices in a quest to nurture her spiritual life. Her personal story grew and changed to place in context her vulnerability to illness and what she was discovering of God in the process of healing. She had not lost the grace she had experienced three decades earlier under the willow tree.

We cannot see what we do not look for. It is easy to pass by a Mary on the street. Our culture teaches us not to stare, not to make eye contact, not to get involved. It is easy to see only the symptoms, but not the soul, of a Sylvie, someone whose behavior is "off," whose words are bizarre, whose clothes may look weird.

But the Psalmist got it right: God is ever present. Look again at the stranger, the outcast. God is there. Look again at those who are ill, those who have nothing but the rags they are wearing, those with eyes full of sadness, those who are exhausted by the struggle simply to make it through the night. These are the first and foremost among us, the least by the world's standards—but the treasured companions of Christ.

What do we learn in taking up the cause of companionship with Mary and Sylvie? What do their stories teach us, those of us who are concerned with caring for the soul in the struggle with mental illness, those of us who wish to help someone we love—or someone we might not know very well who happens to come into our life at a time of desperate need?

Our first task is to understand the symptoms of suffering for what they actually are—signs of a mental disorder.

Our second task is to engage and support appropriate treatment.

Our third task is to find and use spiritual resources and practices that strengthen the work of the Spirit and amplify the healing effort.

Our fourth task is not simply to aid in the restoration of the soul, but to actively help expand the soul's capacity to include the reality of illness in the immensity of our spiritual life, and in the wholeness of who we are as persons.

In one of our final conversations, Sylvie raised a challenging question: "It says in the Bible that we are to be perfect as God is perfect. I don't think I will ever be perfect. My doctor says I may need to be on this medication for the rest of my life. It's like I have this awful flaw."

Perhaps we need to ask what it means to be perfect as God is perfect. The perfection of God is not achieved by cutting out and throwing away whatever is spoiled or wrong or broken, wounded or damaged. The perfection of God is wholeness, a taking up of all that has happened and is, and including it as part of life, and working with it redemptively, so that even the worst of experiences, the most terrible and destructive events in our history, become part of an ongoing creation, ever renewed. The perfection of God is inclusive. The perfection of God is all about a love that nothing can deny. God's love and care for our souls is a gift, freely offered, no matter who we are or what we have done. It is the denial of God's grace to the suffering and struggling that is abhorrent to God.

God approaches us no matter what the circumstances of our existence. No matter how challenging our situation, God is there, without price, seeking our well-being. What is unforgivable is to deny this absolute and ever-effective grace and insist that a person must do this or say that, or pay in some way for God's love.

In the fullness of God there is room for all souls, room especially for those of us who are seen to be the least desirable and most estranged, those who are cast to the uttermost edges of the world. God's perfection is to welcome the most unloved and unlovely, and to fashion from our imperfect lives a Godlike beauty.

5

COMPANIONING BREEZY

Around noon one day in the early spring, I was passing through Plymouth Church in the heart of downtown Seattle on my regular rounds when I saw an unfamiliar man at the piano in the first-floor lounge between the sanctuary and the church offices. The man's unwashed clothes, windblown hair, and well-worn bag on the floor suggested he was homeless. He played pretty well—solid rock chords, a nice rolling rhythm in the bass, and a pumping melody. I listened from the doorway as he finished the piece. He paused, then played again, first just a few notes and then a longer song, apparently his own composition. Eventually he stopped and turned his head toward me. I approached and introduced myself. He called himself Breezy.

I had seen Breezy on the street a few days earlier, walking with a slight hitch and treating his left leg tenderly. He kept his distance from others and occasionally ducked into a doorway if there were too many people on the sidewalk. Now, however, in the safety of the church lounge, he felt secure enough to start a conversation with me.

The church graciously let him come in and play from time to time, and we began to meet on a regular basis. We went for a simple breakfast at the nearby Red, White and Blue café, where we could get an egg, toast, hash browns, and coffee for a couple of dollars. This became a weekly routine, and gradually, over our meals, Breezy opened up about himself. He spoke vaguely of episodes in the hospital. He had been on the road a lot, hitchhiking back and forth across the country. He was waiting for a music contract to come through from

Los Angeles. This contract was something quite complicated, involving copyrights and recordings and substantial sums of money. In the extraordinary workings of Breezy's mind, the contract was a reality.

In Seattle, Breezy had been sleeping in a winter shelter, but that closed for the season shortly after we met. The weather was still cold, however, and Breezy moved around a lot at night. The pain in his leg grew worse, but he was reluctant to have it checked out until one morning when I found him on the street, hardly able to walk and willing, at last, to see a nurse. At the clinic, he was diagnosed with a serious case of cellulitis. He was given medication and a respite bed prescription for a shelter.

Eventually, Breezy got to feeling better. He and I walked a great deal together, side by side along the sidewalk, gazing into a store window now and then, stopping for red lights and continuing on the green. More than once, one of us pulled the other back from the crosswalk when a car suddenly turned the corner or sped by at the last instant of the yellow light. We talked a lot, although I mostly listened.

I encouraged Breezy to meet a colleague of mine, Ken, a social worker with Health Care for the Homeless. Breezy agreed, and Ken joined us for breakfast one day. The three of us meeting together repeated itself—our circle widened by one more person—and a ritual was born, Ken eating a malted waffle with maple syrup, Breezy and I sticking with our eggs and hash browns. We kept up these regular meetings for more than a year. Breezy talked, Ken and I listened. Sometimes we just ate in silence. When the Red, White and Blue closed, we moved, along with the waitstaff, to another diner up the street.

Once we met shortly after the streets of Seattle had been filled with protesters demonstrating against a convention of the World Trade Organization. Extremist groups rioted, smashing store windows and setting fire to trash bins and Dumpsters. The police responded with pepper spray and rubber bullets, and for a while tear gas hung in the air. The turmoil deeply affected Breezy, heightening his fear and anxiety. As we sat now in the café, two police officers walked by. Breezy turned to me in alarm.

"Are they starting again? The riots?" he said.

Ken and I assured him the protests were over, but Breezy remained uneasy for some time, ever vigilant lest the trouble begin once more.

The more we met with Breezy, the more of his story he shared with us: the time he stayed in a hospital for a year, the time he actually performed with a musical group, a few fragmentary glimpses into his childhood and family. If we encouraged him, he would usually expand on some episode of his journey. In our little triad together, Breezy grew to take a definite place. He looked upon Ken and me as trusted friends.

One day, Breezy changed his routine and ordered oatmeal. We talked for a few minutes about changes, and Breezy said a word or two about his dreams and hopes. He wanted something more in his life; he wanted off the street, a home, work. He wanted a sense of worth and dignity.

We began to shape a plan. Ken helped with the practical issues; he guided Breezy through the process of applying for benefits and signing up for housing. We both wanted Breezy to see a doctor for an evaluation, but he was wary; Breezy was still too fearful, too distrustful. But he was willing to meet the physician in the context of breakfast, to have him join our small circle of sharing.

The doctor arrived, and we all ordered. We talked, after our usual fashion, about this and that—as happens in an ordinary conversation. Breezy and "the Doc," as Breezy called him, began to get acquainted —common getting-to-know-you questions and answers. The Doc asked Breezy what he liked to do, and Breezy talked about his music. It happened that the Doc played a little guitar, but he said it was more like a hobby; what he did for a living was help people think and feel better. At the end of our breakfast, the Doc invited Breezy to stop by his office and say hello.

Some weeks later, as Breezy and I were walking in the vicinity of the clinic, we stopped in. The Doc happened to be in the waiting area between appointments. We said hello, a brief moment of reconnection that served to bolster Breezy's feeling of security with the Doc. Subsequently, Breezy agreed to an appointment and began a series of regular visits.

Thus, out of very ordinary interactions and courtesies, a circle of care had developed to support Breezy. We were now four: Breezy, Ken, the Doc, and I.

Healing can require time, and it took us more than a year and a half to help get Breezy stabilized. By Christmas of our second year, though, Ken had helped him find an apartment and move into it. Breezy proudly cleaned it every day, shopped and cooked, and kept meticulous records of his purchases each week. Slowly, he joined in fellowship with other residents. He bought a guitar and played it in open spaces around town. He rode the bus to the top of the Cascade Mountains and back. A secretary at the church had given him several sets of new clothes, and he took to wearing a white shirt, tie, and jacket to our breakfast meetings. He found work to do that was meaningful to him and gave him the sense of self-respect he had longed for. He hunted the streets and alleys, looking for items thrown away but still of use.

Breezy loved Christmas. The previous year, he and Ken had driven out to a suburb to see a live Nativity scene, with children and pets. Breezy was particularly delighted to see a real sheep. Now, as he settled into his new apartment, he asked Ken and me in to bless his very own Christmas tree.

We joined him on a morning shortly before the holiday, and I asked if there was anything special or particular he wanted me to include in the prayer.

"A home," he said, "is good."

We blessed the tree and Breezy's home, and prayed for his continued well-being and healing from all that had weighed upon him and caused confusion in his life. We gave thanks for his special gifts: music and a good heart. And we gave thanks that in this world we need not be alone, but have the help and encouragement of others to find our way.

As we finished this small and intimate rite, Breezy led us over to a table by the wall. There he plugged in a computer that he had scavenged and rebuilt, complete with a monitor and printer that he had also repaired. He turned on the switch. Lights blinked. The screen came alive. Breezy tapped the keyboard, and characters appeared on it, letters and icons. The printer hummed.

It did not yet work perfectly—"and it might never," Breezy said —but he was tinkering with it every day.

His delighted grin said a lot. It was one of those moments when Breezy's soul shone forth unmistakably. His Christmas tree, decorated with castaway treasures from the streets that Breezy had carefully collected, evidenced a coming together, a new iteration of life. Likewise, Breezy's computer expressed an inward concatenation, a linking together of many smaller moments into an emerging completeness.

Finally, approaching the New Year, it came time to celebrate the fulfillment of our companionship. For almost two years Breezy and I, and Ken for only a slightly shorter time, had shared breakfast together regularly, and now it was time to say a goodbye. Breezy was well settled in his apartment. He had made a solid transition into long-term care. His recovery was marked by a widening range of people and activities in his life. Our companionship didn't end but evolved into a less-intensive form of support as Breezy's circle of care expanded into a new community. Our breakfasts together grew less frequent, and we agreed that this time of sharing the journey from street to stability had come to completion.

I asked Breezy if he would like us to meet in our usual place for a celebratory breakfast together.

"No," he said, "I've always liked airplanes. I'd like to go have breakfast at the airport, the three of us. Can we do that?"

"Sure," I said. Planes taking off seemed an apt symbol of the work we were finishing.

We drove out to Seattle-Tacoma International Airport and sat down in a coffee shop in the main terminal, overlooking the runways. Jets of all sizes and small commuter planes were taking off and landing, passengers coming and going. The coffee house staff rushed about waiting on the customers at this busy hour.

The three of us talked and enjoyed our meal. As our breakfast concluded, Breezy smiled, looked around the table, and offered a kind of benediction.

"Someday, when we are old men together," he said, "we'll go to the top of the Space Needle on New Year's Eve and have dinner there."

It was another moment, a touching one. We are not yet old men, but we shall become so. And perhaps, in the fullness of time, we will meet once more at the beginning of some New Year, at the pinnacle of Seattle's most famous structure, and celebrate, again, past times and future possibilities.

In Psalm 139, verses 14–16, the poet of faith sings the following to God:

> Thou knowest me right well;
>   my frame was not hidden from thee,
> when I was being made in secret
>   intricately wrought in the depths of the earth.
> Thy eyes beheld my unformed substance;
>   in thy book were written, every one of them,
> the days that were formed for me,
>   when as yet there was none of them.

In the imagination of God and the vast potential of the Spirit is all possibility. From our earliest and most intricate beginnings, we are God's beloved offspring. Our ever-emerging lives are cradled in the Maker's hands. In every unfolding occasion, in each shaping moment, at every level of our becoming, the Spirit of God creates the day's horizons and offers to us a range of relevant possibilities. The

Spirit does not impose an agenda upon us, but invites our growth and well-being, in body, mind, soul, and community. The Spirit does not dictate each step or outcome, but graces every emerging moment with the treasure of love and freedom.

We are constantly being born out of the past with its undeniable set of realities, and the Spirit works with those realities. The Spirit also understands the influences pressing upon us in the present. The Spirit honors our capacity for choices and decisions, our struggle to make connections, to assess and interpret, to act with feeling and thoughtfulness in the world with others.

The Spirit holds the web of relationships that supports our lives. From the beginning, the Spirit of God knew Breezy and understood the intertwining genetic lines that formed his earliest emergence in this world. The Spirit was (and is) aware of the complexity of interactions that shaped Breezy's infancy, childhood, adolescence, and young adulthood. The Spirit anguished at the first evidence of a malfunction in Breezy's brain, the symptoms of his thinking gone awry.

In the book of Genesis we read, "God said, 'Let us make man in our image, after our likeness . . . ' " (Gen. 1:26). God, working through the Spirit, created us in all our complexity.

What if that decision had gone differently? What if, in the process of Creation, God had made us merely stone replicas of what a person might be—like, say, the famous monumental carvings on Easter Island? That verse in Genesis might read, "Let us carve humankind from rock and set the creations in rows on a hillside, silent, where the rain and the wind and the long years will wear them back to dust." Or perhaps the design might have been to sculpt us in perfect bodily form, as the great artists of classical Greece did, without life—and without the complications and sufferings we have always known.

But we are not made of stone. We are made, as the Psalmist says, "little less than God" (Ps. 8:5). And we do have our complications. Neither our intricate wholeness nor our uniqueness can be accurately modeled by even the most advanced supercomputer and the most elegant software architecture.

When Breezy succeeded in rescuing and repairing his small computer system, he achieved something that hinted at what had been happening in his life slowly over the period of his healing. Likewise, the lights that brightened his Christmas tree, the hard-scrubbed cleanliness of his floor and kitchen, and the enthusiasm with which he played his new guitar—all signaled the Spirit's efforts in the life of his soul.

In companionship, the Spirit moves to support the healing and growth of the soul. Sharing the human journey together is vital in everyone's life, but it is especially crucial in the life of persons beset by illness, hardship, grief, or tragedy. Being present to a soul tormented by fear, buried in depression, or bouncing wildly from one extreme emotion to another can be trying. But companionship provides a way. Companionship is the vehicle through which God heals. Through companionship, the gifts of the Spirit are made real.

Companionship, in this sense of acting in collaboration with the Spirit, is not a task or assignment. It is a *calling* rooted in our common humanity, arising out of an inherent care and concern for one another. The aim is not to fix things; it is simply to *be together,* to be present for one another. Companionship is an *unfolding and growing relationship,* a way of sharing the world together.

But what does such companionship mean, specifically? How do we "do" companionship, *be* companions?

Companionship can be described in terms of four practices: offering hospitality, walking side by side, listening, and accompaniment. Let's consider these in detail.

OFFERING HOSPITALITY. The root notion of companionship comes from the Latin *cum panis,* with bread. We are familiar with the stories of Jesus breaking bread with his disciples, feeding the five thousand, supping with friend and stranger alike. One of the most compelling images of life shared with God is the "great feast" to which all are invited—especially the outcast, the marginal, and the wounded. Sharing even the most humble meal can be a sacred act. In all known cultures, enjoying food and refreshment is an expression of kindness and friendship, a sign of grace and true welcome.

Companionship begins as we offer hospitality. It begins as we stand or sit with each other side by side and look out together upon the world in solidarity. Companionship begins in noting a barely sounded utterance, hearing a catch in the throat, sensing a word wanting to be spoken, listening as an inarticulate emotion or thought makes itself known. Companionship begins in small acts of accompaniment, walking together a few paces, saying goodbye with a promise to say hello again—and some sense that we carry one another as part of our lives when apart.

There is another definition of hospitality relevant to the practice of companionship: creating together what Henri J. M. Nouwen, in his book *Reaching Out,* calls "free and friendly space for the stranger." We seek to establish a space that is sacred in the personal sense, a space where we listen to the other person's story and find the connection to our own. Within this space, each of us must feel safe to be who we are, to receive and accept each other without an ulterior motive and without passing judgment. Like breaking bread, creating shared space has its scriptural precedent. Think of how many times Jesus welcomed the wounded, invited the children to sit with him, welcomed the company of outcasts, called people to sit at the table with him, and talked with strangers even those scorned by his own people—without casting judgment on them.

The same applies if the "stranger" in our midst happens to be a loved one. Someone we've known while healthy can become a stranger to us under the impact of a serious mental illness. We thought we knew the person, but now he or she is acting in a way we don't understand. We may find ourselves rejected if we approach the person as we always did and if we judge them by the standards of our former relationship. The challenge is to build a new relationship— to start where the other person is today, to create a shared space in which the other person feels safe and free to trust.

Breaking bread together was an important part of the supportive relationship Breezy, Ken, and I shaped, and creating a safe, free, and friendly space was crucial to gaining Breezy's trust and helping him move toward healing. But companionship with another who is wounded, fragile, and constantly on guard may need to start slowly. It took time for Terri to allow me to help her get the medical care she needed; it took months of streetside encounters for Mary to trust me even enough to say one word to me.

One of my interns with the Mental Health Chaplaincy began sharing a bench with a troubled man at a station in the bus tunnel that runs beneath downtown Seattle. The man came there each day and sat unobtrusively at the end of the platform. Over several visits, the intern and the man began to speak. The intern decided that the next time he saw the man, he would invite him to have coffee at a little café up on the street level, near the stairs that go down into the bus tunnel. The intern came back and reported that the man declined.

"Do you think he felt safe leaving his bench and going with you?" I asked.

"Perhaps not," answered the intern.

I said, "You might try asking him if you could bring him some coffee."

The intern tried that, and the man accepted. It was a big step forward in their emerging relationship.

Offering hospitality asks of us that we appreciate how difficult it may be for another to take even a first step with us. We begin with the smallest of graces, the little mercies that foster a safe and supportive space.

WALKING SIDE BY SIDE. In companionship, we position ourselves not across from, but alongside, the other person. We stand next to each other against the wall, or we sit together on the curb. We look out at the world and share what we see, respectful of each other's viewpoint. In this stance, it becomes clear that we are on a journey together, fundamentally equals, neither of us ultimately better or more powerful than the other.

Adopting a side-by-side stance does not mean that we never look the other person in the eye and talk face-to-face, and it doesn't mean that we never lead if someone is open to a new way. It means, rather, that we avoid the *confrontational* and the *directive* approaches. We do not blame, and we do not give orders. We are not an accuser, interrogator, or judge; we are not there to march ahead and expect the other person to follow us, nor do we stand behind and push. Each of us has our own viewpoint, our own experience and interpretation of what is real and important.

When Breezy and I walked the streets of Seattle together, we walked as companions; we walked as equals.

It was Terri, the woman we met at the cathedral in the opening chapter of this book, who first made this point clear to me. One day, she and I entered a doctor's office for an interview and evaluation. The physician sat behind a large and imposing desk and invited Terri and me to take chairs in front of the desk facing the physician. Terri, however, refused to sit down.

"What's the matter?" said the doctor.

"I don't like this arrangement," Terri said.

"What arrangement?" the physician asked.

"Your desk and chairs," Terri said.

"What would you prefer?"

"I'd like you to bring your chair over here and sit with us," Terri said.

"Fair enough," the doctor said.

We sat together in a semicircle, a little human trinity, seeking to make sense of our lives and the world, each of us possessing gifts helpful to the whole.

LISTENING. It is an incredible gift, to listen. Can you recall the last time someone simply listened to you, without interruption or commentary, without starting off on their own anecdote or jumping in with judgment or advice? It is so rare. But deep listening is at the heart of a companionship of the Spirit.

Often it is hard to catch all the details or even understand what someone in the worst phases of a brain disorder is saying. At times with Breezy, for example, his mind would run off in its own direction, his speech was jumbled, and it was hard to follow what he was saying. With others, there are frequent pauses or long silences; their concentration may lapse; their memory may fail; the words may simply stop. Very often they cannot easily acknowledge or express their feelings, their hurts, their worries, or their fears.

I have a few phrases that will sometimes help in such moments: "Can you tell me more?" Or simply, "Help me understand." It is at just such times when listening is most difficult—and also most important. Showing care and being open are the key to communication.

Approaching others with great openness is also important. The other person may ask me whether I agree or see things the way he or she does. No matter how strange or off the mark the person's perception might be, I make an effort to accept and understand their reality. It usually doesn't help to challenge or argue, and I try not to tell someone "you are wrong" when the person's brain is creating an experience that feels very real to the person. Instead, I will say that my experience is different. I will ask the person to elaborate, to tell me how she or he is feeling, to share with me what the experience means to them and where it is leading them.

In such moments, what is most real is the actual sharing, the reality of our presence together, and the fact of our conversation. Listening is not about winning a verbal contest, but about hearing who others are, what their mood is, and what they understand to be happening in their life. In listening, we are coming to the truth, moving together toward a common ground.

And as we listen to the other, it's important to listen also to ourselves. What Breezy shared with me evoked feelings, memories, and thoughts of my own. I too have had dreams and fears; I too have traveled a difficult road. Listening to ourselves as another speaks helps us realize that we have far more in common than we realize. We are connected at levels and in ways we do not always immediately realize.

The contemporary German thinker Jürgen Habermas has suggested that every utterance is an invitation to conversation, and every conversation is an opportunity to seek and share deep truth. Breezy first spoke to me through the chords he played on the church piano; his music was a sound offered for those who wished to hear and respond.

One time Breezy's music was getting to me. He was playing so loudly that I felt myself shaking with the relentless pounding of his bass. I asked him to stop, and he did.

"Too bad," he said.

"How so?" I asked.

"Because in a few more bars we get to the anchor chord, the place where it all ends and begins and goes on forever. When we get there, man, it's not just me playing. I know that."

When we listen, we learn. Breezy experienced the Holy in his own particular way: the anchor chord, where it all begins and ends and goes on forever. We all experience the Holy, the movement of the Spirit and the life of the soul, in our own fashion. Sometimes we find the words to describe it. We draw on the wisdom and language of those who have gone before us in faith. We turn back to ancient stories and songs, the witness of scriptures, the traditions of covenant, creed, and celebration shaped down through the ages. And sometimes we do not have words for the experience.

"Sometimes," as Breezy once put it, "there is no word. There's just sound. Or silence. Or maybe light."

Whether it is words, sound, or silence, we must listen if we are to hear it.

Listening can bring unexpected gifts. There was the time, for instance, that I came upon an elderly stranger, Charlie, who was homeless. We got to talking, and he told me he had lived long ago in Cheney, a small community in eastern Washington state. As a youth, he had gotten his first job on a wheat ranch from a guy named Martin Mickey.

"He was a good guy," Charlie said. "He cared about people. He was always reaching out to help."

My mouth dropped open. Martin Mickey was my grandfather. He

had died before I was born, but on my twentieth birthday his widow, my grandmother, wrote me a letter introducing me to him—"your Grandpa Mart," she called him. And here on the street, some decades later, was a living connection to the grandfather I had never known in person, but whose influence had passed into me through pictures and stories and the love of those closest to him.

Suddenly it was I who was being companioned—by Charlie, a man who had been a stranger moments earlier. But Charlie was not a stranger; he and I had a connecting point. And now he was giving me an unexpected and memorable gift. In Charlie's words I experienced my grandfather's presence.

Thus it is that, in listening, we not only give; we also receive.

How do we listen effectively, so that we truly connect, truly share, and truly learn from the other person? Here are seven principles that can help us get there:

1. Listening is a deep gift. Learn to listen without commenting or advising, and make sure to honor pauses and silence.
2. Listen for the feelings and themes of life that are being shared.
3. Listen not just to the other person, but also to yourself.
4. Take care when responding, and invite the other person to elaborate.
5. Listen (a) over time and (b) in the context of community; there is always more to be revealed.
6. Listen for faith, the words of hope, healing, growth, and potential.
7. Listen for the story of the soul—for how the pieces fit together, for where and how the individual story is part of the larger and greater story, for wholeness.

What I am describing is the gift of *spiritual listening*: listening for our connectedness, our common ground, the deepest realities of which we all are a part. Spiritual listening is being recognized more and more as a critical skill for clergy, but it is also a useful skill and practice for lay ministry—and, indeed, for anyone who wants to be a companion to persons struggling with illness or misfortune. Spiritual listening recognizes that we are all members of one family and that the truth of who we are is to be found over time together, and in community.

This is what spiritual listening, as a practice of companionship, aims for: We seek to *understand who we are,* each of us as persons. In the course of companionship we listen for the language of the soul, even (and especially) in the midst of illness.

There is a language of the soul for which we should all listen especially: the sacred story that we each have to tell, the story of our journey toward wholeness. These are our stories of healing and salvation. We each have a faith narrative, a confession, a testimony, a reflection, a religious history. The deepest gift of spiritual listening is the capacity to listen as another person speaks the story of his or her soul.

ACCOMPANIMENT. Companionship, finally, involves the practice of accompanying one another. It can mean helping a person get to an appointment on time, apply for benefits or housing, or pick up and pay for a prescription. It may involve getting on the bus, sharing the ride, finding the right office, walking in the door, taking a number, sitting in the waiting room, approaching the reception desk, talking with the clerk, being there through the interview, following along with the questions that are being asked, helping remember what is supposed to be done next. In my work, the most basic form of accompaniment is going along with someone in person to a shelter, to the clinic, to the hospital or emergency room, or simply to carry out some fundamental tasks to meet a daily need.

Once I spent all day with a man who was in a manic episode of bipolar disorder. I knew he had spent some time in a hospital previously and that he probably needed to go back in for treatment, but he was in no mood to do so now. He kept on the move constantly, and we must have covered a good fifteen miles around the city, but I felt it necessary to be present with him if he decided to go to the hospital—or if his condition escalated to the point where he and others were unsafe.

"I can't force you to do anything," I told him, "but I'll be with you to help if I can."

"I don't need any help," the man said.

But he didn't tell me to leave, and so I stuck with him. Several times we reached the top of steep hills, both of us out of breath, and I suggested that he consider a rest in the hospital. Late in the afternoon, he stepped into the men's room of a department store. I waited in the corridor, ready to take up the pilgrimage again. He didn't come out. Finally, I went in and found that the rest room had two exits. He had taken the other one and gone on his way.

I was disappointed; I thought I'd lost him. But the next day, I heard from two friends of his. He had come to their apartment and asked for their help, and they took him to the hospital.

We should not expect to measure the act of accompaniment by an immediate outcome, but rather by its value as a spiritual practice. It is an act of faith, an outward sign of our belief that we are never alone. It is a sacrament central to the healing process. Accompaniment is an act of hope, a belief in promise and possibility, trusting that the Spirit will support our journey toward wholeness. Accompaniment is powered not by my agenda or your agenda or anyone else's specific blueprint, but by *agape,* the Divine Love that knows no end and comes to us unconditionally.

To sum up, the practices of companionship are to:

- offer hospitality, creating a free, friendly, and sacred space for the stranger;
- walk side by side, looking out at the world together, honoring each other's unique gifts and perspective;
- listen carefully, in community and over time, to hear especially the language of the soul and the story of hope and wholeness in us each;

- accompany one another, both in practice and in Spirit, on a healing journey so that, together, we experience recovery and grow toward wellness.

These practices of companionship are fueled by God's love, the gentle and supportive presence of the Spirit providing hope and care in every moment.

Locals and tourists alike enjoy Seattle's Pike Place Market, where farmers and fishermen have sold their wares for a century, and hundreds of merchants offer specialty foods, flowers, comic books, funky clothes,. handcrafted jewelry and pottery and wooden flutes and knickknacks of all sorts, and where one must stay out of the way when, in a time-honored ritual, a six-pound salmon or a wet Dungeness crab chosen by a customer flies through the air on its way from the display counter up front to the scale and wrapping counter. Throughout the market, musicians and balloon artists and mimes, buskers and street performers of all kinds, share their gifts with strangers and regulars for tips. Amid all this activity, the fine thread of God's love brought a young man named Danny into my life.

I met him outside the market, just south of its main entrance at the corner of First and Pike. He stood on the sidewalk and played the air guitar, invisible and inaudible to all but Danny. His clothes were worn and bedraggled, his hands chapped and his face and limbs lean, but he vigorously strummed a tune whose chord progressions only he understood, jigging his foot in time to his own personal beat. Passersby walked a wide circle around him. He made no contact with them; he had no hat or box open before him, sought no reward for his silent performance.

I watched Danny for a while, then went forward and said quietly, "Interesting music."

Danny glanced my way and nodded. His hair stuck out in clumps from his head, and he sniffled loudly with a heavy fall cold. He kept on playing and then finally rested.

I leaned against the building near him. He, too, relaxed a bit against the concrete, and we watched the world move by.

The next day I brought a couple of take-out coffees, and when Danny took a break, I offered him a cup. He looked surprised, but he accepted the coffee and gulped it down.

We talked just a little, Danny mostly in monosyllables: a yes or no, a nod of the head. He appeared unable to summon up any details about himself or his situation.

Several days later, when he took a break, I asked if he wanted coffee again and he agreed to go with me to a nearby café. As we stood at the counter, I asked him what he wanted, thinking he'd say "black" or "with cream."

Danny read the list hanging behind the counter and, in typical fashion for coffee-crazed Seattle, said to the clerk, "A hazelnut latte, please."

On this day and at this moment, Danny was in a small window of clarity. The vagueness was gone from his eyes. His speech was less halting. His distractedness lifted briefly, and he was able to share a piece of his past. Noting that the café we were in was called Juliet's, he recalled that, in high school, he had acted in a Shakespeare play.

"Where was that?" I asked.

"I'm not sure." He paused for an instant but then said, "Canada."

"How did you happen to come here, to Seattle?"

He told me he'd hitchhiked from Vancouver. When I asked if he had any family or friends in Seattle, he said, "No, no one."

And then the curtain dropped. The act ended, and Danny reverted to the role he played alone, on the street.

Danny and I continued to meet. We broke bread, and I listened. One of his symptoms was an unreliable memory, not uncommon among people with his illness; occasionally a small piece of his past would occur to him, but there were many other times when he remembered nothing, or only a fragment of an event. In cases like Danny's, it is sometimes hard to tell whether the person truly cannot remember or simply does not trust anyone enough to open up about himself. As a relationship builds, however, this can change. The person slowly develops a sense that the listener can be trusted and will allow himself to reveal more. It's a part of the recovery process.

Thus, over time, I learned bits and pieces of Danny's story. One thing he told me was that he had lived in a group home, but left it back in January. It was now November, and as the days grew colder and rainier, I encouraged him to consider spending his nights in the downtown shelter. Danny agreed. I introduced him to Ken, who had his office there, and eventually Danny began visiting the psychiatrist on the Health Care for the Homeless team. I sat in on the initial visits.

In December, Danny said he wanted to go home. I called a colleague at St. James Methodist Church in Vancouver, B.C., a church that runs a transition shelter, and the St. James staff offered to help. Two days before Christmas, Danny sat in the front seat of my old Volvo and we drove north from Seattle.

Two hours later, we were at the border, where the Canadian customs officer asked for our identification papers. Danny had none.

"He's homeless," I said through my open window to the customs and immigration officer. "We've been working together in Seattle. The St. James Shelter in Vancouver is waiting to assist him."

"Could you please park the car over there, and you and the gentleman come with me, sir." It was not a question. The officer pointed to a parking area next to the customs building.

Inside, Danny and I sat in front of the officer's desk. I told him what I knew of Danny, which was really not much, and waited nervously as the officer turned to Danny. I worried that Danny might shut down under the pressure of questions from a stranger, but he didn't.

"Where are you from, son?" the officer said to him.

Danny gave him the name of a town and added, "That's a suburb."

"Of where?" asked the officer.

Danny told him the city.

The officer had more questions—was Danny born there, what was his father's name—and Danny answered them all as I sat, amazed.

The officer excused himself and left us in the office to wait for him to return.

"That was helpful," I said to Danny. "I'm glad you were able to remember that."

"Me too," said Danny.

After some minutes, the officer returned. He smiled at Danny. He had found Danny's birth records and located his parents.

"I found them in the phone book," the officer said. "No one's home, but I'm going to let you in. Good luck to you." He gave me the number.

That night, thanks to the staff at St. James, Danny went to sleep on a bus heading home.

In the meantime, I drove back to Seattle and called Danny's parents. A woman answered, and I asked if she had a son named Danny.

"Yes," she said. "He disappeared almost a year ago. We don't know where he is."

"He's been in Seattle," I said. "He's been getting some good help."

"Thank God," said Danny's mom. She began to cry. My voice broke a little, too, as I told her the details.

"Danny's going to be home for Christmas," I said.

The life of the soul is thoroughly relational. Our spiritual identity comes together as we are held and helped by others, by family and friends, by all who offer to help us learn and heal, by all who accompany us and share in our journey. Thus hospitality, a side-by-side stance, deep listening, and accompaniment are the basic practices of a companionship that seeks to welcome, honor, recognize, and support the soul of another.

Why is it so hard? So often we define each other by a particular detail, rather than appreciating the wholeness we each are. Our alert systems, our worry-and-wary capacities, can cause us to focus on the strange, the unusual, or the negative. A person regards us with a wild expression. He smells bad. She talks in a way that doesn't make sense to us. But who, really, is that person? How do we get past the surface appearances—behavior that is caused by illness and compounded when the world turns its back on the marginalized soul—and how do we come to recognize the whole person, intricately wrought in the image of God?

By sharing that person's journey. When people share a journey together, miracles happen—not miracles in the sense of magic, but miracles in the biblical sense: unexpected moments of grace, of healing and restoration; visible, tangible, believable moments that give us hope.

We are, all of us, miracles, every one of us birthed from God's tender presence in the world. Consider the Christmas story. It is one thing to read Luke's account of Caesar's call for a census of all the inhabitants of the empire, and to hear how Joseph and Mary found themselves in Bethlehem, she about to give birth, with nowhere to rest or sleep, and were finally given refuge; and there, in the humblest of settings, in an ordinary human child, the gentle presence of God came into the world and became known to us.

It is another to discover that God's gentle Spirit is at work among us two thousand years later, still present in the difficult times, active in our everyday lives, caring for the miracle that is each human life and soul.

6

CREATING KARL'S CIRCLE OF CARE

Karl's brother called me from Denver. Karl was being released from jail; could I help him get connected with the care he needed? I asked for a few details and learned that Karl had been homeless for most of the previous twenty years, following his discharge from the army, that he had been diagnosed with schizophrenia or some combination of schizophrenia and bipolar disorder, and that he had a drug problem.

I hung up and drove straight to the county jail, hoping I hadn't already missed Karl. More than once I'd gone to meet someone being released and found that they had already been let out of jail in the middle of the night with nowhere to go.

This time I was in luck. I stood in the jail's prisoner-release area, a large interior space with a bare floor and no windows. A security elevator nearby led to offices and prison units. The release door opened, and through it stepped a smallish, middle-aged man with thinning hair and a bewildered look on his face. He was wearing ill-fitting hand-me-down clothes.

I asked if he was Karl and introduced myself as a chaplain. I said his brother in Denver had asked me to meet him. "I think he would like to be here himself," I added.

"John?"

"Yeah, John," I said. "Would you like to get something to eat, or a cup of coffee?"

Karl hesitated and glanced around that cold space, with its sturdy institutional fixtures. The only colors in the room were on two snack and soda vending machines. Eventually, he looked back at me and said, "Okay."

We stepped out into the autumn air and walked to a nearby diner, where we sat in a booth, a Formica-topped table between us. A waitress promptly plunked down two mugs of coffee. Karl took his cup in both hands and leaned against the vinyl back of the bench, staring around the room at the dusty, acoustical-tiled ceiling and the dated soda fountain advertisements on the walls. Like Karl, the diner seemed to be stuck in an earlier time.

When the waitress returned and asked what kind of toast Karl wanted, he stared at her, then at me, and turned in confusion to the menu.

"White? Whole wheat?" the waitress offered.

It was a simple decision, but Karl was not processing it.

"White okay?" the waitress asked.

Karl nodded. I was struck by how even small things seemed daunting for him in this new environment.

As we ate our eggs and hash browns, I asked Karl about himself and slowly put together a few more pieces of his history. He had joined the army as a teenager. After his release, he held down a few jobs, living in a shack for a while as a junkyard guard or pulling down day labor, but nothing that lasted. He struggled with alcohol and drugs. He was hospitalized a few times for brief periods, and while at the state hospital he had received medication.

Karl was arrested initially for resisting an officer who found him wandering the streets. Karl's recollection was that he had somehow ended up in jail after fighting with some fearsome attackers. He believed they continued trying to get at him in jail and attempted to poison his food. He was transferred from jail to the hospital and, eventually, back to the county jail for release. The day that I met him, he had nothing but the clothes on his back—no money, no medications, no home.

As we talked, Karl relaxed a little. He had a sense of humor and came across as a lonely and basically gentle soul. His memory was poor, and his story came out in fragments of here and there, characters met long ago and scattered events, some of which made little sense. He spoke tersely and tended to summarize the past in blocks of time: "I was young." "I was in the army." "I was on the street." Every now and then, he drifted off, staring away into some middle distance between now and the past and whatever was to come.

I asked Karl how his experience in the hospital had been and how he felt about the medications.

His first response was, "I don't know." However, he told me a little about how scared he felt when he was arrested and that maybe he had been doing some strange things. After a while at the hospital some of his "strangeness" wore off, and he thought maybe the medications helped with that.

I said that there was a clinic nearby where we could walk in and get some help, both with medicine and in getting his life together.

He smiled and spread his hands out, empty palms up. He said, "I don't have anything."

Thus began what turned into a convoluted quest, taking Karl and me through a month-long maze of bureaucratic barriers of the sort that, all too often, frustrate and exclude those in need. Karl's quest for help illustrates how difficult it can be to secure help in our highly fragmented system of care.

Our adventure began just after 8:00 a.m. when we arrived at the county walk-in clinic at the Harborview Medical Center. The receptionist greeted us and asked Karl a few basic questions—name, address, income, insurance, and whether he had ever been seen in the clinic before. Karl answered as best he could. He was given several forms to read and sign, one having to do with patients' rights and another consenting to treatment. These two forms puzzled and confused him, but he signed them and sat down to wait for a screening interview.

A mental health professional took Karl through about twenty minutes of medical and mental-health history questions, an inquiry into his current concerns and difficulties, and a brief mental status exam. The MHP told Karl that he did indeed appear to have some serious mental health issues, but noted that he was not in an acute episode of illness or in an emergency condition. The MHP suggested that Karl apply for Washington State public assistance and Supplemental Security Income (SSI), and then return when he had medical coverage.

At around ten fifteen, we walked into the downtown office of the state Department of Social and Health Services (DSHS) and took a number. A half hour later, Karl's number was called. At the reception desk, we asked for help in applying for assistance and health benefits and were given a six-page form to fill out. The form was meant to screen out anyone who was not disabled or financially eligible for assistance. I helped Karl through the questions. There wasn't much to report on the lengthy page that asked us to list all assets and income—stocks, bonds, treasury bills, life insurance, burial benefits, railroad pension payments, debts owed to the applicant—but Karl resisted checking a statement affirming that he was unable to work.

"I want work. I can work," he said.

"I know, Karl," I said, "but you've had some health problems, and this is to help you get some support until you're on your feet."

I managed to persuade him that he would not be able to get work and earn enough immediately to afford the healthcare he needed. He completed and signed the application for assistance, and we returned to the desk. The clerk thanked us and asked us to wait again.

Around eleven thirty, we sat in a small booth, talking over the counter with a financial worker. She noted that Karl had received Social Security income in the past. Before proceeding further, she asked us to go to the local Social Security office and get a letter stating what benefits Karl was currently receiving.

Karl said, "I've been in the hospital for two years."

The financial worker said Karl would still need a letter from Social Security stating any income he was getting. She thought he might still be on the SSI program, or eligible for it.

We walked into the Social Security office at about twelve fifteen and took a number. When Karl's number was called, we approached the window and talked with a clerk who looked up Karl's Social Security status.

"Our records show that he is receiving veterans benefits," the clerk said.

"I've been in the hospital the last two years," Karl said.

"How much?" I asked.

"It doesn't say," the clerk said. "You need to go to the VA for that."

The clerk directed us to the Veterans Affairs office, which was located in the same building but accessible only through a separate entrance outside. Sure enough, around the block was another door with a small sign that said "Veterans Administration," and in still-smaller letters, "Homeless Veterans Project." This looked promising.

Karl and I climbed the stairs, walked down to the end of the hall, entered the waiting room, and stood in line for the receptionist. He looked up as we approached and said, "Hi, what can I do for you?"

"I've been in the hospital," Karl said. "I don't have any medicine."

"Are you a client here?"

"I'm a veteran," Karl said.

"What's your name and ID number?"

Karl gave his name and I took out the Social Security number we had just gotten for him at the Social Security office.

"The computer says you're a vet, but nothing about being a patient here."

"We're trying to get a letter stating Karl's VA benefits," I said.

"I don't know anything about that," the clerk said. "Maybe you should talk to one of the counselors."

Karl and I waited about twenty minutes, and a counselor came out. I was glad to see that he was someone I had worked with before. He introduced himself to Karl and we sat down in his office. I gave the counselor a brief overview—the state hospital, the release through jail, the need for medications, the trip to the walk-in clinic, the referral to the welfare office, the trip to Social Security, and finally the referral to the veterans office we now found ourselves in.

The counselor closed his eyes for a minute and then said, "There's not much I can do. This is a PTSD [post-traumatic stress disorder] program. We don't take walk-ins and I can't help you with a verification of benefits. Let me call and see who can do that for you."

Karl and I sat quietly while the counselor dialed a number and had a brief phone conversation. After he hung up, he said, "You need to go down to the Federal Building, Veterans Affairs office. Ask security, they can direct you to the right floor."

This was a different VA office a mile away. We walked there, were screened through the entrance to the Federal Building, took the elevator up to the VA office, and passed through the double doors into a large open space to a reception counter with a small sign that said "Information." Here, a now-familiar ritual took us through a brief conversation with the receptionist and a quick referral to a counselor, who led us to his desk and listened as Karl explained that he needed medicine.

The counselor looked a bit confused. "I can't help you with that. That's something you would have to go to the hospital for."

I explained the referral from the walk-in clinic to DSHS to Social Security, the side trip to the VA program outside the Social Security office, and the suggestion that we come here for verification of Karl's VA benefits. The man nodded, asked Karl for his ID number, and spent a few minutes searching on his computer.

"It says his files are in another state," the counselor said.

"What does that mean?" I said.

"Well, it means you'll have to talk with a benefits specialist here and he'll have to get the file transferred to our office. No one's here at the moment. I can have Kathy make you an appointment."

We returned to the receptionist's desk and got an appointment for the next day.

As we were about to leave, a man in shirtsleeves came through the double doors. Feeling by now desperate, I asked the man, "Are you a benefits specialist?"

Taken aback, the man stopped and said, "Yes?"

"I'm a chaplain," I said. "And I'm working with this gentleman."

I quickly introduced Karl and explained the situation.

"Come on back," said the man.

We followed him to his desk. He got Karl's basic information and fed it into the computer.

"It looks like his files are in Texas," he said.

"I lived there," Karl said to me.

"Can you tell us what kind of benefits he has?" I asked.

"Just a minute." The man clicked the computer keys for a while.

"This is interesting," he said. "Karl gets fifty cents a month. It says here that every quarter, a check for a dollar fifty is sent to the supervisor at the state hospital to help cover his expenses there. Are you supposed to be in the state hospital, Karl?"

"No, I left there," Karl said.

"Can you give us a printout or something that we can take back to Social Security and use at the DSHS office?" I asked.

"I'll have to get his file transferred to this office. That may take a couple of days. Is he a resident in Seattle now?"

"Right now he's homeless and needs medicine."

"I'll get his file transferred, and maybe you could take him up to the VA hospital. They have a mental health program there. Just ask when you get to the front desk. They can direct you."

We got in my car and headed for the VA hospital, a massive, labyrinthine medical complex on top of Beacon Hill. The front desk clerk gave us directions to the outpatient mental health center, buried deep within the building's second floor. Finding it required the help of several kind strangers, but after some minutes we were in the Behavioral Health waiting room, explaining Karl's situation to a medical clerk. She listened carefully, her expression gradually deepening into a frown. She said she was sorry, but that the only way patients could be seen in the outpatient clinic was by going through a screening and evaluation process starting in the emergency room.

Late in the day now, we made our way to the ER. We sat waiting our turn to present at the desk. A young man welcomed us and led us through the procedure, entering Karl's name and ID into the database. The man noted Karl's lack of address and uncertain benefit status, and asked us to wait for the nurse.

Soon a nurse weighed Karl, took his temperature and blood pressure, and then sat us in a small examining room. A social worker arrived to take a brief history. Karl was vague; he had been in the hospital but couldn't exactly remember what medicines he had been given. He talked about being homeless for many years and mentioned a friend who had once taken him in for a while. The social worker asked him questions about various symptoms. After about twenty minutes, the social worker glanced over his notes.

"Karl's illness doesn't appear to be service-related," the social worker said to me. "He'd have to go on a waiting list for the outpatient program. That would probably take six months, and even then it would be pretty minimal. Our case management services are restricted only to those who have had at least two psych hospitalizations. It's basically designed to prevent rehospitalization. Your best bet would be to try the crisis service at Harborview."

Exasperated, I said, "That's where we started this morning."

"I'm sorry," said the social worker. "I don't know what else to tell you."

It was now 6:30 p.m. and the walk-in clinic was closed. Karl and I had talked with fifteen different people in seven different programs that day.

Karl's eyes seemed to ask, *What now?*

I sighed, smiled tightly, and said, "Come on, Karl, let's try to get you a place for tonight."

From the ER, I called the emergency shelter downtown. They had an open mat and said to bring Karl on in. I explained to Karl that this was a place where he could make a base for the next few days. It helped me that there would be others there who could be a part of his care team.

Several times that day, Karl had asked me my name, where we were going, or what office we were in. In the car now, on the way back downtown, he turned to me and asked once more, "What's your name again?"

I smiled and said, "I'm Craig, the chaplain."

Karl smiled back at me. "I think you may be an angel."

We parked near the shelter, and I accompanied Karl up the stairs to the registration window. A young woman greeted Karl and registered him. Then I took him in and introduced him to the supervisor and the floor counselor. We made a plan together to have Karl wait the next morning, with some coffee on hand, until I could pick him up and resume the process of getting him enrolled in care and treatment. Thus, three more new faces—and an eighth program—finished our day together. There was, of course, more to come.

Karl and I continued the journey over the next several days. We took a full-pay appointment with a private physician, who made his evaluation, filled out the necessary form needed for state assistance, and prescribed a two-week course of medication. We collected the paperwork from the VA benefits specialist and a letter from Social Security stating that Karl was not currently receiving benefits. We returned to the DSHS office with this documentation, met with the financial worker, and set up a meeting with the disabilities specialist. Karl was granted state public assistance, and in anticipation of his being approved for SSI from the Social Security Administration, he was granted Medicaid benefits to pay for community mental healthcare treatment. At last, Karl was getting the care he needed.

If Karl's story seems complicated, imagine how it might have gone had Karl, who could not remember my name and may not have understood exactly where we were at any given moment, tried to navigate the maze of bureaucratic procedures by himself. Imagine, if you will, how hard it is for a person who is homeless and wrestling with hopelessness, fear, or great confusion, or difficulty with memory, intense anxiety, hallucinations, or delusions, to even begin to negotiate alone the steps toward care.

I recall another man, Jack, whom I accompanied to a clinic for a screening. The screener performed a mental status exam.

"Do you know what day it is?" the screener asked.

"Thursday," Jack said. (It was Tuesday, actually.)

"Do you know what time it is?"

"Four," said Jack. (It was ten in the morning.)

"Can you tell me where you are?"

"Husky Stadium," Jack answered. (He was referring to the University of Washington football field, which was miles away.)

"Some people hear voices that no one else hears. Do you hear voices?" asked the screener.

"Yes, they are telling me I shouldn't be here," Jack said.

After the mental status exam and interview were concluded, the screener, an MHP, said to Jack, "You have symptoms we can help you with. You are eligible for services here. What I want to do is set up an appointment for Thursday at ten o'clock. You'll meet with our intake worker and, if we can schedule it, we'll have you meet with a doctor or nurse to talk about medications, but that may not happen until next week. I'll write you out an appointment slip."

I noted to the screener that Jack had difficulty orienting to time and place; he was experiencing symptoms that had made it very difficult for him even to come to the clinic in the first place. I added that he was homeless and afraid to use a shelter. I asked if it might be possible to consider admitting him to the hospital, where he could be safe, get a thorough evaluation, and begin the process of stabilizing on medications.

The screener said, "I don't know if he would meet the criteria for hospitalization." To Jack, he said, "Would you go to the hospital if we could arrange that?"

"I don't know what to do," Jack said, looking at me sadly.

Exactly. Jack had reached a point on the streets where he was stuck, pushed and pulled by the forces of illness but still open to help. Every step was a struggle for him. On the walk to the clinic we had stopped numerous times, and at the door, Jack froze, reluctant to go in. He was neither gravely disabled nor a danger to himself or others—the criteria that would usually open the door to the hospital—but he needed help, and he was willing to accept it.

The image of Sterling Hayden, wanting and in need, came to my mind, but this time I knew what to do. Jack's story has a happy ending. I stayed with Jack, pleaded his case forcefully to the right people, and he was admitted. Jack was on his way to care and rehabilitation.

It can be surprisingly hard to get someone into the hospital. I had learned that, first with Sterling years earlier and now with numerous other sufferers. Once, for example, a pastoral colleague called me downtown at nine o'clock on a winter's night, distressed by the condition of a woman he'd found huddled in the back doorway to City Hall. The woman, Shelly, had a history of mental illness and hospitalizations. Now she was seven months pregnant, shivering, and coughing badly, but in a state of euphoria and grandiosity in which she saw nothing at all wrong with her situation. She was certain that as soon as people recognized her many gifts and talents, and her plans for making Seattle the capital of a country she called Cascadan, she would be fine. I told her I was concerned about her cough and the cold weather, and asked if she would be open to going with me to an ER to get checked out.

Shelly agreed and got into my car. The warmth inside began to calm her shivering; once inside the emergency room, she was able to lie down wrapped in several blankets and drink a cup of hot tea. The medical staff diagnosed her with bronchitis and then waited while the mental health professionals made their evaluation. She was experiencing mania, they said, but she was not a "good faith" voluntary patient. They said she probably wouldn't stay in the hospital if she was admitted; she would take off after a day or two, against medical advice. She was too ambivalent to commit herself to care and treatment, and she didn't meet the criteria for an involuntary admission because she wasn't a danger to herself or others and she wasn't gravely disabled.

"What about the pregnancy?" I said. "It can't be healthy for her to be sleeping outside, pregnant and with bronchitis."

I was told that if the bronchitis developed into pneumonia, then she would "meet criteria," but for now she would have to go back to the street. I asked if she could stay in the waiting room, but that was not permitted. During a previous episode of mania she had become belligerent; she was cited for trespassing and barred from sitting in the ER.

At that point, Shelly insisted on going back to City Hall and spending the rest of the night in the doorway. She asked me to leave. I did, after saying I would check on her in the morning.

Next day, I found her in the main entrance. One of the staff at City Hall was trying to help her, but Shelly was irritated. I invited her to one side of the lobby, and we talked. Her cough was worsening, but she was becoming more insistent on completing her mission. She calmed down somewhat and sat on a bench while I went off to consult once more by phone with the MHPs. A team came and evaluated Shelly. They couldn't assess her bronchitis there in the City Hall lobby, but they agreed to go ahead with a legal summons, requiring Shelly to come into the county ER within twenty-four hours for a checkup or be involuntarily committed to the hospital for up to three days for an evaluation. When served with the summons, Shelly tore it up and said she was just fine.

I tracked her for the next twenty-four hours as her condition continued to worsen. She wasn't eating much. Her cough was more severe and her mania escalating. She stuck around City Hall, and when the twenty-four-hour waiting period was up and she continued to deteriorate, I called the MHPs in again. The team came and called for an ambulance. I took Shelly's hand for a moment as she lay on the gurney, waiting to be rolled out of City Hall. She looked up and, in one of those moments of clarity that can come from the health deep within, gave a little nod.

This was the right thing. Shelly herself, flooded with illness, had not had the capacity to seek help on her own and was hostile to care. But in our companionship, in her fullness as a person, in this relationship of souls, care was possible—not in perfect form or in the most timely manner, but it was nonetheless there, waiting to be realized.

*　　*　　*

"Lo, I am always with you," says Jesus in the last verse of the Gospel of Matthew: a personal, human-being-to-human-being expression of the infinite and unceasing, tender Spirit of care that holds us each, no matter how complex and difficult our circumstances.

In companionship, we accompany another as a living embodiment of the creative, nurturing, and grace-full love that is present in every life. When I met Karl at the jail, the Spirit of God was already at work amid his struggle. The Spirit was seeking to foster Karl's inmost well-being by creating around him a circle of support; seeking, that is, to knit Karl, in company with others, into a fabric of care. I happened to be available and present at the moment when the circle of support began to form.

This is how I saw my role in Karl's journey with the Spirit: I wanted to honor Karl's own capacity to experience, explore, initiate, and decide—to reinforce his fullest sense of becoming whole. Wherever possible, I wanted to join the activity of the Spirit and amplify it. If I could help prompt a thought, clarify a choice, open up a direction, assist with Karl's memory, or encourage him to persist, this was how I could be of use. In the act of accompaniment, I sought to understand how the Spirit moved as, together, we—Karl and I—were embraced by healing and recovery.

All of us are part of the larger spiritual network in each other's lives. All that we embody or reflect of the Spirit in our actions, words, and decisions has an impact on those with whom we are sharing the human journey. When that journey brings us into companionship with someone suffering from mental illness, our role requires the utmost respect and sensitivity for the other person, and an intense consciousness of the internal confusions, blockages, and barriers presented by neurobiological disorder and psychological struggle.

The work of healing and recovery is not left to us alone, nor is it all loaded on the shoulders of companionship for us to bear together. I cannot overemphasize how important it is for us to recognize that the care and support of a person with serious mental illness hangs on the cooperation of a community of people, a *circle of care* that brings together people of different skills who can share the tasks of caring. Faith in God and the work of the Spirit are important—but faith and love alone are not enough. Mental illness is a *medical condition* that, nearly always, needs to be treated through medical means. Those of us who would aid and support someone struggling with mental illness—whether it is a loved one or a stranger—must understand that appropriate medical care is essential to ease suffering and prepare the ground for health and wholeness.

There are those who question the efficacy of treatments for mental illness, as well as those, like the churchgoers who shunned Sylvie, who believe symptoms of mental illness expose a lack of faith—or the presence of a satanic force within the person. To my way of thinking, such attitudes are far from the truth and, indeed, harmful not only for a person's health but for the life of the soul. I believe that, when it comes to illness and healing, the work of God is not simply a matter of faith but depends on human companionship and care, and the collaboration of those to whom God has given the skills and wisdom of medical science. The circle of care so needed by one who suffers from serious mental illness must include qualified practitioners of the healing arts.

In psychiatry, the physician moves from diagnosis to prescription to treatment and the evaluation of the treatment, constantly refining theory and practice. When a practitioner makes a diagnosis, he or she seeks to understand the organic conditions and processes at play within a person's brain and in the body as a whole. The practitioner also seeks to understand the developmental journey of the individual self, the inner and relational psychological world, the conscious and unconscious realms of thought and beliefs the person carries within. Through diagnosis, a doctor, nurse, or other trained professional attempts to understand how the surrounding world affects the patient's being and considers how the social powers and forces shape patients' lives, both as individuals and in relationship with others. A thorough diagnosis also includes a view of a person's potential, their maximum capabilities.

A deep diagnosis will go beyond the physical, neurological, and psychological dimensions and consider also the realm of the Spirit, for it is here that all of us come to understand the ultimate context of our lives. It is in the realm of the spiritual that we may experience our most intimate moments of faith and find our core identity.

Effective care and treatment, leading to the fullest healing and recovery, depends on a diagnosis of depth and richness: Will this particular medicine or therapy be the best or most effective? Is there a particular combination of care that will be especially helpful? What is the likely and expected course of recovery, and what needs to be in place to support this person's maximum well-being?

When the symptoms are complex, the diagnosis may suggest the need for consultation and collaboration in treatment. We may wish that one physician alone can cure us, that a single counselor will restore our course and balance, or that one simple procedure, pill, diet, or discipline will bring us health. It might be so if we were simple robots—some wires, a battery, and a lightbulb that flashes on and off. But we are far more. We ask for quick and easy miracles, but we have difficulty appreciating the incredible miracle each of us already is. Healing is often a team effort, recognizing and honoring the complex creation we each are.

As for the question of medicine versus faith, I see no conflict between the healing science of medicine and the art of practicing our faith. Dr. Andrew Borland, a psychiatrist and colleague, once expressed it this way: "The patient and I do all we can to understand the origins and nature of the illness. I use every bit of knowledge and experience I have to help us shape a plan of treatment. We work with each other to adjust the care. And then we wait for healing coming toward us." The process of healing is aided by both medicine and ministry; each contributes its particular gifts of care.

Contemporary Western culture has a tendency to draw a boundary between our physical form and our spiritual lives. This is not true of certain Eastern cultures—and it was not always true of Christendom. In the early Christian community, there was no great divide between body and spirit, between ministry and medicine. Among Jesus's disciples was Luke, the physician. But today, many people find this issue a source of conflict. Hospital patients are sometimes torn between their faith in God and following the recommendations of a medical team.

I've heard it expressed in a number of ways: "If I take the medicine, will I be denying God's power to heal me?" "I want to be faithful and let God heal me."

The scriptures tell us that healing can come to us in many ways. In my New Jerusalem Bible, Chapter 7 in the book of Wisdom, verses 15 and following, affirms that God gives to humankind the gift of knowledge, both "understanding and technical knowledge," and teaches the "structure of the world and the properties of the elements," "the natures of animals," and "the mental processes" of human beings.

In the thirty-eighth chapter of the book of Ecclesiasticus, we read that "the Lord has brought medicines into existence from the earth and the sensible person will not despise them" (v. 4). Further, the Lord "uses them [medicines] to heal and relieve pain, and the chemist makes up a mixture for them" (v. 7). Ecclesiasticus tells us that the "doctor too has been created by God" (v. 1) and that "the physician has the art of healing from the Most High" (v. 2). Ecclesiasticus teaches that God works through all who give care.

When we are confronting depression, bipolar disorder, schizophrenia, and other mental disorders, there is no easy solution. The issues can be complicated. "What is wrong with me?" patients ask. "What is happening with me?"

We have bodies that can weaken. We have brains that can malfunction and need strengthening. We can become deeply troubled in mood and emotion. We can lose heart or, at the opposite extreme, feel invincible. We have minds; we think and imagine, and sometimes our thoughts can go off track, our perceptions can become strange.

We are souls, with spiritual depth and capacity, but we can lose our way. Our spiritual life can become a struggle.

We may need healing in one or more of these areas of our lives and need the help of family, friends, and neighbors. I want each person to have a team of support—doctors and nurses, a counselor, a social worker, a spiritual guide, family and friends—a circle of care that helps each of us to gain strength, be at peace within ourselves, think clearly, and be whole.

There is nothing in scripture or faith that forbids us to avail ourselves of the full care of the community and the rich range of help and support available to us from many fields of knowledge. Healing at its best is a function of community.

I was called one morning to an inpatient psychiatric unit. A middle-aged man, a refugee from a war-torn country in Africa, had been admitted to the hospital several weeks before, deeply depressed. His recovery process had begun successfully, thanks to the compassionate response of the staff, an antidepressant medication, the help of a counselor, meeting and sharing with other patients, and pastoral care visits. Now it was time for him to be discharged; his bags were packed and plans were in place for him to stay with an immigrant family from his homeland. But he refused to go.

The man, Eli, greeted me warmly in his room and thanked me for coming. He expressed how grateful he was for the help he had received, mentioning several staff by name. He said he was feeling much better, like his old self. But he still refused to leave his hospital room.

"I cannot go," he told me. "I must see the priest."

"Why is that?" I asked.

"In my village," he said, "when someone has been very ill and left the community, the priest must say a blessing before the sick person returns to the village. That way everyone knows to welcome you back. The blessing is very important."

Sensing that I was not equipped to give Eli what he needed, I called a priest of his community and asked for his help. The priest arrived, carrying a small leather case, and he and Eli exchanged greetings. The priest took a vial of holy oil out of his case and, singing a prayer, he anointed Eli's head and cheeks with the oil. Still chanting, he embraced Eli with a great hug, and then stepped back. Eli smiled, picked up his bags, and went home.

Would that all of us might carry such a human touch and blessing, whatever our illness, that we might be welcomed in the community and the door opened to our healing need.

For this is the work of the Spirit: to foster our well-being within and call us to each other's aid in the journey toward wholeness.

7

GRACE

At twenty-four, Ally appeared to be on her way to a successful business career. She had done well as a sales rep, earning several bonuses in the past year. But then something happened. She started talking nonstop about the "mountain of God." She missed work and spent hours at a time in church. Just after Christmas, her sister took her to the emergency room. Ally was diagnosed with bipolar disorder. She stayed in the hospital for a short time and was released with a prescription for medications to help stabilize her mood swings.

Around Easter, her illness once again intensified and the level of her medication proved insufficient. She resumed her vigils in church. As her mood escalated further, she felt herself called to a revolutionary and divine mission. She was an invincible, militant angel patrolling against the forces of evil, which she believed were associated with particular cars and vehicles. Energized by this mission, she went for days without sleep. One day she stationed herself on the shoulder of Interstate 5, shouting at drivers to stop and get out of their vehicles. She stepped out into the roadway and a driver swerved to avoid her. Brakes screeched and other drivers cut their steering wheels to keep from hitting the cars in front of them. Fortunately, there was no collision and no one was hurt. Soon a state patrol officer arrived, assessed the situation, and arranged to have Ally taken to the hospital.

Once more, care and an adjustment of her medication restored Ally to stability, but she now struggled to understand her illness. After the first manic episode, she had left the hospital thinking it had all been a brief, onetime aberration; she hoped she was cured. The second episode forced her to confront the depth of her vulnerability and the possibility of a lifelong journey with her illness. She went home with serious questions and a haunting sense of guilt. She worried for her soul and her place with God.

Ally's pastor referred her to me, and I met her in a neighborhood coffee shop. Around us people sat and talked, read the newspaper, discussed business, planned projects. Ally sat nervously, her face pale. She clutched an old, battered backpack.

"What if I had caused an accident?" she said. "What if somebody had been killed?" She fiddled with her empty paper coffee cup, slowly peeling the handle from the side. "I didn't decide to walk out on the freeway, like I was making a conscious choice."

"I don't think you had a choice, Ally," I said. "Your brain was malfunctioning. Your usual self was offline. You were living in an illness world."

"But it seemed real," she said. "I felt like I was in a terrific battle. I had this mission. It was like being in one of those futuristic movies, you know, where civilization is destroyed and people are trying to survive. Like *Road Warrior* or *Blade Runner.*"

For Ally, it *was* real, as real as being in a swarm of wasps, as real as a World War II battle. More real than the images of *Road Warrior* on the screen: villains in armored trucks with flame throwers and grenade launchers; the good guys defending themselves with whatever they could salvage from the ruins around them.

Ally glanced around at the other patrons in the coffee shop. She had twisted the handle of her paper cup until it came off. "I'm a freak, Craig. But I was really caught up in it all."

"Ally, your brain created a kind of movie," I said. "You were acting a role in your illness story, but not one you chose."

I shared with Ally a little of my own story, particularly how it had felt for me as I steered toward the bridge abutment. She found it hard to believe that I, too, had been mentally ill. Ally felt isolated and vulnerable. Situations and sensations that feel completely real don't make sense—sometimes even to the person experiencing them—and yet Ally, and many, many others, are swept up into the version of reality created by their malfunctioning brains, alone to fight their battle, alone with their tears.

Repeatedly in our conversations, Ally said things like "it wasn't really me" when she described standing on the freeway, shouting at passing drivers, and yet she wasn't completely sure. She knew she had been there. The memory continued to cause her embarrassment, shame, and guilt.

I offered an explanation that seemed to help. "Ally, you know how actors play roles in a movie or TV show? Imagine you're playing a role—Grace, say, in an episode of *Will and Grace*. It's just a part. You give it your all while you're in front of the camera, but the part you play doesn't define you. Similarly, the part you play in an episode of mental illness doesn't define you. Because *you,* Ally, are far more than any one or two episodes in your life, even those two extraordinary episodes of mania. You are far more than your illness self."

This is the truth—the truth about people battling bipolar disorder, depression, schizophrenia, and other serious illnesses, and the truth about us all. We are each a whole life story that is greater than any given moment and much more than our illnesses, wounds, troubles, or sorrows. Who we are, in turn, is part of a still larger story, the story of the world and human beings and eternity. We are a part of this planet and the universe, a part of worlds we can't even begin to imagine.

It is in the context of our place in the universe that we can talk about the great issues of good and evil. It is in terms of our whole life story that we can make sense of our responsibility and destiny as persons. We need to understand the nature and power of illness in our lives before we make judgments. We need to explore the larger reality of our existence and go to the heart of life together before we condemn ourselves or others.

It took Ally a while to absorb this. She and I met together over a number of months, continuing to explore her moral concerns and her questions of blame and salvation. An important part of her healing was her growing understanding of her disorder. Over time, Ally was able to frame her illness story with increasing self-compassion and share her experience with others. She was active in a support group of fellow patients, who helped her understand that her journey was not, as she had supposed, unique. She began to speak in churches and in the wider community, taking part in an educational effort to dispel myths and address the stigma of mental illness. Her candor about her experience, the way she owned her vulnerability to mood swings, her willingness to talk personally and share what she had learned on her journey—all served to encourage others who were struggling, and their family members as well.

As she healed, Ally explored anew her spirituality and faith. Her natural capacity for faith had been compromised by her illness. She realized that her malfunctioning brain had produced distorted religious notions and bizarre images, and as we worked together, she was relieved to discover that she had not lost her faith during those episodes; it was still available to her as a source of support for her recovery and wholeness.

Again, it is not uncommon for psychiatric symptoms to take a quasi-religious or pseudospiritual form. While serving my first parish in Massachusetts many years ago, I took a young man to the local mental health center on Easter night. He believed he was Jesus Christ, and he had tried to kill himself in order to rise again. The inpatient mental health floor was full, and there were already two "Jesus Christs" there; the staff did not think it would be helpful to add a third. We were referred to a regional hospital that had a larger psychiatric section.

Such experiences do not arise primarily from the activity of the Spirit, but from powerful, neurobiological processes. Our spiritual capacities can be deeply disturbed in the course of illness, but they are not ultimately lost. We may not be "in our right mind." We may "take leave of our senses." But the Spirit is at work with us always.

Consider Walter. Believing he was following a biblical imperative to "drive out the moneylenders," he crashed his car into a building. While recovering from both his physical injuries and his manic episode, Walter, like Ally, struggled to understand what his responsibility was: How did his acts count before God? Where was he headed now? What was the fate of his soul?

One afternoon, I accompanied Walter and several other patients on a group outing to an art museum. Walter stopped in front of a painting that depicted a partially ruined castle tower and courtyard. The painting was empty of human life, save for a woman hunched in the lower corner of the courtyard against a high wall, one solitary being in an otherwise desolate setting. Walter was drawn into the picture. He saw the ruined building and thought of the ruination his crash had caused. He identified with that lonely soul in the courtyard, lost and isolated, with no way out.

Then he noticed a small doorway set into the courtyard, leading to the landscape beyond. Through the doorway the viewer got a tiny glimpse of the world beyond: a small garden, green fields, water.

Walter's face lit up. "The door will open," he said.

Walter saw in the painting a distillation of his own experience. He had had a part in a ruinous situation. But he could now put a frame around that painful episode. He had been ill, but he was not locked into his illness picture, nor was he condemned to forever pay for what his illness self had caused. Illness was a part of who he was, but it did not define him, and it need not determine his future absolutely. He was on a path toward health and life in a reality that lay beyond his illness.

Ally, too, had felt the isolation. Slowly, she was finding her way out of the desolate landscape as she and I worked on that larger story of her life, the deep questions of her purpose and meaning. We traveled together as she explored the basic concerns of her soul, a search that would be ongoing long after my ministry of companionship with her concluded.

Ally's religion—one filled with rich statements of faith, awe-inspiring cathedrals, and a formal liturgy of beautiful chants and ancient rituals—provided much that was helpful to her healing process. She loved the High Holy Days, the masses and the magisterial rites, and the support she felt from a great sea of souls in worship. However, she also felt at times overwhelmed by the formalities of her church and longed for a simpler experience. Within her larger church family, she discovered a smaller congregation that practiced a more contemplative form of worship. She adopted a "Brother Lawrence" approach to her faith, after the model of a seventeenth-century French monk who felt the presence of God as strongly in the monastery kitchen as he did while kneeling at the altar. Ally found in Brother Lawrence's "kitchen spirituality" an encouragement to experience the gentle touch of God in the ordinary dimensions of daily life.

There is no one spiritual path or set of practices that I prescribe. However, I have often found that a spirituality of the simple and down-to-earth can be helpful for those who have experienced the abyss, the grandiose, or the bizarre, or have struggled with great anxiety or compulsions. And that was true for Ally.

Little by little, Ally's confidence grew. One day as we were sitting at our usual back table in the coffee house, she said, "I don't think I'm guilty."

She had been keeping a spiritual journal, and she shared with me now something she had written while watching an ambulance pass by her apartment. She had wondered about the person inside, if it was someone who had been in an accident—or was it, perhaps, someone like her who had experienced an acute episode of brain illness and needed help getting treatment?

"And I thought of something else," she said. "I suddenly had an image of God in the back of the ambulance, holding the patient's hand. God is where people are hurting, not in a courtroom somewhere, waiting to pass judgment."

Ally and Walter, like many who experience mental illness, felt humiliated. They lived in fear of judgment and sought relief for their estranged, abandoned, and shattered souls. Ally in her vision of the ambulance and Walter in his glimpse of the doorway in the courtyard received an immeasurable mercy.

Mercy is a primary gift of the Spirit. Mercy nurtures reconciliation and renewal in our lives. Mercy touches the hurt in our lives. Mercy reaches out and embraces our feelings of shame and embarrassment. Mercy acknowledges our grief and guilt. Mercy tempers judgment with wisdom and understanding. Mercy expresses the love of God, gentle beyond all measure and yet of such strength that nothing can separate us or negate our lives and worth.

Mercy flows from the compassion of God. God's heart is touched by our struggles, more deeply than we can imagine. God feels our every pain, suffers with us, and holds our lives as treasured. In God's care, our souls have eternal value.

In the face of mental illness, we are called to be merciful. The first act of mercy is to be present, to hold and share in the woundedness of our brother or sister. We are called to be compassionate, to understand rather than to judge. We are called to *live reconciliation,* to *be deeply with* our neighbor. In mercy, we realize the fullest truth of who we are as persons and experience a wealth of grace and hope. In mercy we meet as fellow sufferers, no one of us more deserving of care than another. What I offered Ally in her struggle was not words, doctrine, prayer, or penance; it was not a rite or practice. What I offered was my own fragility and vulnerability, to be shared with hers.

Let's return to Karl, whom we left in chapter 6 as he was making slow progress toward stability. Karl was well along in his treatment for schizophrenia when I ran into him at a drop-in center. We spoke for a few minutes, and he caught me up on his living situation, his part-time job, and his medication, which had recently been adjusted, but his illness was persistent and his journey had been frustrating for everyone involved in his care.

Karl presented a complex picture of symptoms. At first, his fears were what stood out; he worried, for instance, that someone was poisoning his food. A newer-generation medicine effectively reduced his paranoia and helped restore Karl's capacity to think more objectively and confidently. Because substance abuse was part of his chronic problem, he met regularly with a chemical dependency counselor and attended meetings of Alcoholics Anonymous and a Narcotics Anonymous group.

Despite his commitment to working with the chemical dependency program, Karl relapsed several times. These relapses affected his health, and they also put him at risk for losing his housing. There were times when he missed appointments with his treatment team and then showed up intoxicated and in a buoyant mood, spilling forth with the details of new friends, new loves, and high hopes for the future. When the effects of whatever street drugs he was using wore off, Karl readily acknowledged that he had slipped. He worked on the triggers, worked on relapse prevention, and worked his 12-step program. But it was hard sometimes for his family and team to hang in there with him and keep up the support.

Karl relapsed again, but this time he came in the first day of his binge. His mood seemed euphoric; he spoke rapidly, and some of what he said bordered on the grandiose. But he had barely begun to use. His treatment team began to suspect something they had missed before: his "high" was the result of something more than the use of street drugs or alcohol. His self-report suggested that his mood had swung upward before he started using—he was already highly animated and increasingly uninhibited. The care team thought it quite possible that, in addition to the schizophrenia they had already diagnosed, Karl might be subject to bipolar disorder, and that this second disorder of brain chemistry underlay his drug use.

As Karl's mood escalated, he became increasingly oblivious of consequences. He didn't think he would come to any harm. He gave away money. He was victim to anyone who offered to help him have a good time. He'd let anyone crash in his room. Karl's capacity to consider alternatives became less and less available. Illness was overpowering his healthy brain functions—the basic operating network each of us needs to make good choices. Once he started using or drinking, that part of Karl's brain that was conditioned for years by the regular use of street drugs and alcohol kicked in quickly. Intoxication then added its own disturbances and distortions.

It is one thing to stay the clean course while your mind is sound. It is another to grapple with not just one but *two* devastating brain disorders—and be vulnerable also to drug and alcohol abuse. Such was Karl's plight.

Karl's care team put him on a mood-stabilizing medication. The symptoms of mania abated. His emotions leveled. He got his feet on the ground and his head into the world with others again. His hyperactive romanticism faded. His craving for excitement resolved into an enjoyment of more ordinary pleasures: a swimming expedition, a movie night, visits from family and friends. He was far better equipped in body, heart, mind, and soul for the pilgrimage of recovery and growth. He was given a gift of mercy and understanding.

We cannot make the journey alone. None of us. We are made for life together, made for community. Those of us blessed with health and wealth may be tempted to forget that. We may want to believe we are self-made and assume that we have succeeded through our individual merits alone. We might look down on others, believing that those who have not achieved what we have are less motivated or less virtuous. We may come to accept as normative a world that provides grand homes and attractive neighborhoods for the well-to-do, and slums and streets of endless suffering for the poor and disabled. We may even unconsciously have a view of heaven as a place of many mansions for the deserving, but no room for those who in this world are marked as flawed.

Illness—and especially mental illness—confronts us with the unavoidable truth of our frailty and finitude. Illness underscores our fundamental dependence on the love and help of others. Ally, who counted herself among the upwardly mobile prior to her illness, never imagined that she could fall so completely apart and so need those who formed the circle of care to support her healing.

None of us arrives in this world of our own will and effort. Our very survival, in the earliest years, is utterly dependent upon the assistance of others. We grow into a degree of maturity and autonomy. A few of us may even develop the skills to live off the land, on our own as a lone wolf, but very few can survive for long without connecting to others. Even the desert fathers, third-century Christian hermits who lived in the Egyptian desert, relied on a support network that occasionally brought them supplies of life's necessities.

Our full identity as selves and as souls emerges only in relationship. A pure, unalloyed, independent existence is, in the end, nothing. We exist because we are cared for. We *are* because we are *loved.* And we have a responsibility toward those with whom we share this world. We are created for human interaction; we are meant to have an impact on one another, designed to give and receive, to shape and be shaped.

From the beginning, each of us has been held, surrounded, and supported by others at every moment. Once I sat in an airplane across the aisle from a mother and an infant. The baby flailed his arms and kicked his legs, turned his head and cast his eyes this way and that, smiled and gurgled. His mother reached for his tiny hands and let them tap into her own. His little legs thumped lightly upon her stomach. Their eyes met first in this moment and then in that. She grinned and laughed to his smile; she oohed with concern when his mouth puckered and his forehead wrinkled. Child became child in the orbit of his mother, and this new mother became mother in the orbit of her child. That elemental scene of love and play, mother with child and child with mother, affirmed that we are sculpted in mutuality; we are shaped in our responsiveness to one another.

Individually, we are fragile and vulnerable. In infancy and childhood, in illness and when we draw our final, feeble breaths, we know this truth: that we live by grace, not by our own grit and good works. It is when we recognize our limits and our need for others—indeed, *honor* our limits and our need, and honor also the sensitivities and vulnerabilities of others—that we begin to appreciate the call to responsibility, the call to care for one another.

Time and time again, the scriptures call upon us to love one another, and to love especially those most at risk among us: the ill and
frail, the widow, the orphan, the infant, the poor, the oppressed. In
the end, this is every one of us. We are all in some way wounded,
stumbling, lame, uncertain, insecure, and in need of tenderness. We
may armor ourselves emotionally, move about in motorcades, put our
hands to the levers of power, live in pomp and ostentation, and bask
in the light of prominence among our fellow humans. We may see
ourselves as first and best. But in the actual count, we stand side by
side with our most troubled neighbor, neither better nor worse, but
fully equal as humans.

Asked for an illustration of our responsibility to each other, Jesus
told the story of the Good Samaritan (Luke 10: 29–37). This is one
of the most familiar passages in the Christian Testament, but it bears
repeating with one or two points of emphasis. A man lay by the side
of the road after having been beaten and robbed. Two important and
busy persons passed him by, but a third man, a Samaritan, a person
from a despised minority, stopped to help the man in need. The
Samaritan gave the man first aid and got him to an inn, where he
could heal.

It is no coincidence that, in this parable, woundedness responds
to woundedness and suffering recognizes suffering: the socially
wounded Samaritan helps the physically wounded man. The final detail, often overlooked, is also important. The Samaritan does not act
alone. He takes the man to an inn, where the man recovers in the company of others—the innkeeper, neighbors, and the community.

Jesus did not only teach tenderness and compassion, he lived these
qualities. His life stands as an example of how we are called to reach
out to the weaknesses and sensitivities of others. He touched those
who were sick and broken. He welcomed those whom others reviled.
He affirmed the worth and dignity of the lowly. He revealed his own
limitations and vulnerability when he was arrested, convicted, and
crucified by those in his community who found in his message of love
a threat to their power and authority.

Jesus moves in mercy, loving because he is loved. His tenderness is the tenderness of God, the gentle Spirit of God embodied in the world. Like Jesus, we are called, *by Love,* to love.

God's tenderness is perfect. In tenderness, God fully embraces all that we are—including all that is broken and flawed, all that falls short of our highest potential. In tenderness, the Spirit heals and redeems what the world judges worthless or despicable. In God's tenderness resides an infinite mercy and an eternal, ever-mutual, unbreakable relationship with us.

This unceasing Spirit of love provides the energy for our profoundest acts of responsibility toward one another. Empowered by the Spirit, we enter relationships in which our core nature as persons is made manifest. We experience the full reach of love, and we explore the mysteries of grace and mercy operating at the most intimate levels. By opening to one another and by sharing our need for care, we create together moments of sacredness. We receive the gifts that make for wholeness and salvation.

One day in the hospital a medical resident approached me, concerned about a patient, Morgan, who was under treatment for schizophrenia. Morgan had been progressing well as his medications gradually reduced his delusions and paranoia. But he had handed the doctor a letter, filled with descriptions of plagues and battles, apocalypse and doom. I read the letter and recognized the language of the last book of the Christian Bible, the Revelation of Saint John.

> And the fifth angel blew his trumpet, and I saw a star fall from heaven to earth, and he was given the key of the shaft of the bottomless pit; he opened the shaft of the bottomless pit, and from the shaft rose smoke like the smoke of a great furnace . . . Then from the smoke came locusts on the earth . . . In appearance the locusts were like horses arrayed for battle; on their heads were what looked like crowns of gold; their faces were like human faces, their hair like women's hair, and their teeth like lions' teeth; they had scales like iron breastplates, and the noise of

their wings was like the noise of many chariots with horses rushing into battle. They have tails like scorpions, and stings, and their power of hurting men for five months lies in their tails. They have as king over them the angel of the bottomless pit . . . (Rev. 9:1–3, 7–11)

I told the physician that, as far as I could see, Morgan was not presenting the return of symptoms; rather, he was genuinely trying to communicate to his physician what he had experienced in the course of his illness. I pointed out that Morgan had penned in an introduction to the passage that read, "This is what my illness is like . . ." In recovery, Morgan turned to the language of Revelation to help him express and share what he had been through.

While healing, Morgan had a gnawing concern. Was his illness, with its vivid, agonizing delusions, meant as a punishment, or perhaps a warning? Was God trying to scare him? Had he done something so vile that deliverance was impossible? Like Ally, Sylvie, and Walter, Morgan's illness was compounded by a sense of condemnation and guilt.

When disturbed, our brains can create a living hell as damning as any scripture or fire-and-brimstone preacher can describe. Our imbalanced brains can take the image of God as a vengeful deity and force it upon us as an absolute, immediate and inescapable, implacable and terrifying. I have come upon souls literally writhing in despair, wrapped in an agony that no words of comfort, reassurance, or deliverance can relieve. Their broken brain has seized upon an oft-told religious theme: the notion of our utter depravity, our irredeemable sinfulness; the notion that only by the payment of some awful penalty can we be made right with God; the notion that only a sacrificial death and the winning of a cataclysmic battle can allay God's disappointment in us and deliver us from the powers of destruction.

The sacred scriptures of many religious traditions contain terrifying stories and frightening images. The book of Revelation in the

Christian Bible is an example, with its scenes of mighty battles, otherworldly creatures, and Armageddon. Revelation can be read as a literal prediction of future events, and indeed, in every age there have been readers who saw specific events in their own time as the beginning of the apocalyptic era described in the text. Others see the book as a collection of symbols and allegories written in code, and seek to decipher its meaning. The strange creatures, the use of numbers, and other elements are interpreted scene by scene and applied to our understanding of history and current events. Still others read the book of Revelation more like a literary work, with a message of encouragement to a besieged and persecuted early Christian Church. By this interpretation, the very strangeness of the book and its visionary, epic form can be interpreted as a way of allusive writing that helped the text get past Roman censors—a language that was meaningless to the rulers of the time, but a source of hope and reassurance to a community under attack.

But I am also taken with the way Morgan turned to the book of Revelation. "This is what my illness was like . . ." Morgan found in this strange and disturbing book a presentation of the world as he experienced it in his illness. He did not take it literally. He did not try to decode it. He didn't read it in a particular historical context. He read and saw John of Patmos, the writer, as a fellow human being whose mind had imagined bizarre and terrible things. However, the author of the book of Revelation was able to put a frame around his experience. He was able to write it down in a coherent fashion. The book had a beginning and end. The book of Revelation also contains themes not only of struggle and destruction, but of hope and wholeness. In chapter 21, for example, is an incredibly tender description of healing:

> Then I saw a new heaven and a new earth . . . and I heard a great voice saying, "Behold, the dwelling of God is with humankind, God will dwell with them . . . and God will be with them. God will wipe away every tear from their eyes and death shall

be no more, neither shall there be mourning, nor crying, nor pain any more, for the former things have passed away." (Rev. 21:1, 3–4)

I believe that these inspired words carry the deepest truth of Revelation, and that the book as a whole is well used as Morgan found it —as a way for us to share both our fearfulness and the ultimate horizon of healing and salvation.

Others, however, have distilled from the book of Revelation a horrific and punishing image of God, which, in its rawest form, is terrifying. One of the most famous sermons in American history is Jonathan Edwards's "Sinners in the Hands of an Angry God," preached in Enfield, Connecticut, on the eighth of July, 1741, and subsequently preserved as a seminal text of the first Great Awakening, a revival movement designed to convert unregenerate souls. I first came upon the sermon in my high school American literature textbook. The text, now readily available on the World Wide Web, uses language still heard in some pulpits today.

The following is an excerpt from Edwards's sermon. Listen to these words concerning sin and punishment, traditional language meant to terrify people into repentance and turn them, in their fright, to God. Hear them as one who is already gripped by great fear in the midst of a severe, persistent mental disorder, cut off from human relationships and barely hanging on to any semblance of reality. Put yourself in the place of someone like Morgan who is seriously ill, and already heaped with guilt and terror:

> The God that holds you over the pit of hell, much as one holds a spider or some loathsome insect over the fire, abhors you... You hang by a slender thread, with the flames of divine wrath flashing about it, and ready every moment to singe it, and burn it asunder;...When God beholds the ineffable extremity of your case and sees your torment and how your poor soul is crushed,...he will have no compassion upon you...He will

crush you under his feet without mercy; he will crush out your blood and make it fly ... No place shall be thought fit for you, but under his feet, to be trodden down as the mire of the streets ... There will be no end to this exquisite horrible misery. When you look forward, you shall see a long for ever, a boundless duration before you ... and you will absolutely despair of ever having any deliverance, any end, any mitigation, any rest at all ... Your punishment will indeed be infinite.

Such sentiments are not unfamiliar to me. I have stood at the edge of the bottomless pit. I have felt the absolute and utter abandonment of God, the near-total absence of the Spirit. I have experienced the sense of being irrevocably lost. This was not the result of a divine plan for my life, but the consequence of depression. In illness, my broken brain told me that I had been dropped from the hands of God forever. In the course of recovery, I have experienced quite the opposite: a Spirit of gentleness and healing that bears us up, eternally.

The terror Jonathan Edwards described is not found in the core teachings of Jesus. Christ offers an open and healing hand, not an iron fist. Christ calls us to commune with him; he does not stand ever ready to cast us into an unceasing suffering. I hate to think what my fate might have been had a pastor come to my home and attempted to "save" me with such threats of a violent damnation. The loving, guiding, comforting, courage-giving, uplifting, healing efforts of the Spirit in our lives stand opposed to the image of a God who is capable of not caring, a God who stands ready to mete out infinite suffering.

I work day in and day out with people who live in fear of such threats. A woman cries in sobbing anguish, "Please tell me I'm not wicked." A man on the street stares at me and hangs his head, muttering, "I'm beyond God's universe." A man on a bench in the rain repeats over and over, "No hope, no hope, no hope."

I have kept vigil at the bedsides of dying parishioners, and comforted family and friends as we said our prayers and goodbyes. The grief can be immense. But I have never sat with anyone in more anguish than Jerry, from chapter 2, when he asked me, "Is there anything for me in this world?"

Once I gave a presentation about my ministry at a large church, and during the coffee period afterward, a parishioner asked me if I saved souls.

"What do you mean?" I said.

"Do you tell the people on the street that if they accept Jesus Christ as their Lord and Savior they'll be saved?"

I paused for a moment, gathering my thoughts in order to respond with care, and then said, "No, I don't do that."

I paused again to consider my words carefully, but before I could continue, the man shook his finger in my face.

"*You're* going to hell," he said.

And before I could answer, he turned his back and left.

A part of me wanted to shout after him, "I've already been there!" I did not.

What I wanted to tell the man was that most of the folks I work with are so frightened, depressed, confused, or delusional that to approach them with commands or threats would be not only meaningless but downright damaging. I wanted to tell the man about Jerry, Walter, or Morgan, already frightened to death; about Mary, Ally, and Sylvie, whose reality had become a living hell; or about myself and my own descent into the hell of hopelessness.

I understand the faith story, the religious picture, out of which this man makes his judgment. It comes out of a particular way of looking at the Bible, a specific framework for the story of healing and salvation. It is not a message that I find helpful for working with souls who are suffering from acute or persistent brain disorders.

And it is not a picture of God that I choose to preach or teach. It is not a spiritual understanding that best serves either a broken brain or a broken world. The God I have experienced is not a Grand Inquisitor who confronts us with the horror of our sins, or a harsh judge who dangles us, on a fearsome day of reckoning, "over the pit of hell, much as one holds a spider, or some loathsome insect over the fire," and decides whether to drop us into the flames or save us. I believe it is the constant work of the Spirit to hold us in love and seek our well-being. I believe the Spirit seeks to deliver us from every form and power of evil, however and wherever it takes shape in us and in our world.

I approach each soul with that trust.

I begin with these most intimate truths: we exist in a web of Creation and relationship that is eternal and unbreakable; the power of healing is greater than disease; the gift of life is greater than the forces of death; and love is ultimate.

Tenderness, not tyranny, is at the heart of our universe.

I am convinced that, in the end, the issue for all of us is not guilt or punishment, but grace. I myself have fallen into the bottomless pit. I have been present with sisters and brothers who are dangling in an eternity of unforgiveness. I have visited men and women who believe themselves to be so sinful that they have attempted to cut off their hands, pluck out their eyes, or take their own lives. I have come alongside neighbors who are screaming and tormented as if trapped in Dante's inferno. I cannot imagine God seeing or seeking such punishment for any creature—ever, let alone forever.

Ignorance, injustice, and evil have very real and potent consequences in the world. We become sick. We abuse our strengths. We mistreat one another, or we are callous in our care. We build on false grounds, commit fraud, lie, and fall far short of the mark in our personal and social lives. We have the capacity for great violence, and we exercise it, as individuals and especially as nations, sometimes subtly or unconsciously, and other times openly and blatantly. We put on elaborate protections and wear all manner of armor; we don the masks of hubris and arrogance, attempting to cover over our fears and weaknesses. But all this is a complex twisting and turning away from what is central in life: the grace-filled activity of the Spirit.

The presence of the Spirit in our lives does not require us to utter a specific set of words, repeat a particular verse or prayer, or affirm a certain creed. There is no one act that we need to perform to guarantee the fruits of the Spirit in our lives. Healing and wholeness, the care and restoration of our souls, a place of honor at life's feast—these are the Spirit's constant, free, and full gifts. Grace holds us each and holds us all.

This is the good news of the scriptures we hold dear in the Christian tradition. This is what Jesus consistently talked about, beginning in his home synagogue in Nazareth. There he read from the prophet Isaiah: "The Spirit of the Lord is upon me, for he has anointed me to bring the good news to the afflicted. He has sent me to proclaim liberty to captives, sight to the blind, to let the oppressed go free, to proclaim a year of favor from the Lord" (Luke 4:18–19).

In parable after parable, Jesus described the realm of God in terms of an unceasing care—the search for the lost sheep, the return of the prodigal son, the story of the great feast, the failing fig tree. In the story of the prodigal son, the father sees his child at a distance and runs to embrace him, knowing only that he who had been lost was now found. Even before the young man speaks, his father is gathering him up and calling for a celebration (Luke 15:11–32, especially v. 20).

Feast and communion are basic images of sacred hospitality and the gifts of the Spirit. In the parable of the great feast in Luke, we read an extraordinary message of God's inclusiveness. A man invites his neighbors to a feast. They beg off, saying they will be out of town or have other matters to attend to. Then the host says to his servant, "Go out quickly into the streets and alleys of the town and bring in here the poor, the crippled, the blind and the lame . . ." and then, when there was still room for more, the host said, "Go to the open roads and the hedgerows and press people to come in, to make sure my house is full" (Luke 14:21, 23).

Jesus lived what he taught. He reached out especially to those who were on the margins, to people others despised, to those who were most broken and abandoned, the lonely and wounded, the unlovely and oppressed. He joined his life with the lives of those who suffered and welcomed all into the tender heart of God.

There is no more powerful story in the scriptures for me than that of Jesus welcoming the naked man running down the hillside toward him on the Gerasene shores. He treats the man as a person of worth and dignity, and he heals him. This is the Jesus I know as a brother and a support in my work on the streets. This is the Spirit of healing that I have experienced, together with those who have cared for me and those with whom I have ministered. This is the tenderness and love I have found flowing abundantly from God.

And what, finally, about the sisters and brothers who have not survived their mental disorders?

Enid and Ben had two teenage daughters, Emily and June. Most people who knew them saw a warm and close family, churchgoers and good citizens who lived in a comfortable suburban house with an attached garage. Few knew that Enid was ill.

Weighed down by depression, Enid stole through the kitchen and into the garage late one night as her family slept. She closed the door between the kitchen and garage tightly, and made sure that the garage door, too, was sealed. She sat down in her car, started the engine, and allowed herself to be asphyxiated by the exhaust. What she did not know was that the garage wall leaked gases into the bedroom where Emily and June were sleeping. Emily survived, but June, like her mother, died from breathing the lethal fumes.

The family was in shock. Grief spread from Ben and Emily to Enid's parents and brother, and their extended family and community. To lose a wife and child, a mother and a sister, was almost beyond bearing. In the emptiness and tragedy, family and friends groped for words of solace and tried to grasp the incomprehensible. And unspoken was the fate of Enid's soul, she who had not only taken her own life, but caused the death of her beloved daughter as well. What possible consolation could there be?

At the funeral, the family's pastor spoke to the grief and to the questions mourners brought in their hearts.

"There is no guilt here," he said. "There has been no fault—only a terrible illness and a great suffering because of it. God casts no blame, but cries with us for our loss. God's arms are open to Enid and June, and they are open to us, too, in this hour and forever."

The Spirit holds who we are in unbroken relationship, keeping us even as this body which has been our home slips away and is no more. Tenderly we receive a new being, a new dwelling, a new life, in a new realm.

The apostle Paul, referring to the body we inhabit, speaks of "this earthly tent." The body we are given is intricate; it develops for months in our mother's womb and matures over the course of many years. It gives us extraordinary capacities. But it comes, for all of us, with a final fragility. The "temple" we inhabit is temporary.

Our identity as persons does not rest in our body alone. Who we are is held, and valued, and lives in a web of compassion greater than we can ever fully imagine. Our souls—our wholeness and fullness as persons—are carried in the constant care of the Spirit. We rest ultimately in the life of God, whose love for us knows no bounds.

There is in the Bible a most difficult story of suicide: the case of Judas Iscariot, who betrayed Jesus to his death and was paid thirty pieces of silver. In the Gospel according to Matthew, we read of the last moments in the life of Judas:

> Flinging down the silver pieces in the sanctuary, he made off, and went and hanged himself. The chief priests picked up the silver pieces and said, "It is against the Law to put this into the treasury; it is blood-money." So they discussed the matter and bought the potter's field to bury strangers in. (Matt. 27: 5–7)

The potter's field as described in Matthew is a last refuge for the alien and the outcast. Tradition suggests that Judas himself was buried there.

I read the story of Judas in dialogue with my own spiritual journey. In the moment of my greatest frailty and vulnerability, when my life hung by a bare neurological thread, I found myself in a potter's field west of Ann Arbor, off the interstate and at the end of a dirt road.

With shards of misfired pieces, and new and reshaped works waiting to be finished in the kiln, the potter's field was a place of both brokenness and creation. It was a place of ending, but also of beginning.

I believe that the tradition which rests Judas in the potter's field communicates a Gospel truth. This most broken of souls is held gently by God, who is shaping us all and forever, anew.

PART III

A Community of Tenderness

The way of companionship leads to new life in the company of others, to the building of circles of care. It is in community that our souls flourish and we lay the foundations of a just, peaceable, and healing world that truly includes the least and most broken among us.

How is healing community formed? The citizens of Geel, a town in Belgium where everyday families take mental patients into their homes, trace their effort back more than seven hundred years. Plymouth House in Seattle, Washington, rooted in the same Spirit that helped shape Geel, is a home where four volunteer companions live with patients who are homeless and come directly from the hospital to continue their recovery. Meeting and treating suffering in the world begins with sensitivity, compassion, and concern for our neighbor and the building of care, community by community.

Part III looks at two community-based programs of care and visits a small country struggling to rebuild its mental health system after a devastating conflict. The final chapter, "Words Are Medicine, Too," explores how our most basic beliefs and the language of faith speak to the challenge of mental illness and help us shape healing and meaningful lives together.

8

DO YOU KNOW THE LEGEND?

In the seventh century AD a Celtic king in Ireland became deeply depressed upon the death of his beloved wife. His grief was overwhelming, and his mind deteriorated to such an extent that he came to see his young daughter, the princess Dymphna, as the reincarnation of his wife. When the king tried to force Dymphna to marry him, she fled Ireland in a small ship and landed on the European continent in what is today Belgium. There she hid from her father and devoted herself to caring for the sick. Driven by his illness, her father pursued her and eventually found her in the small community of Geel, east of Antwerp. When Dymphna again refused to be his wife, the king flew into a rage and murdered her. She was buried in a crypt beneath the local church.

Six centuries later, workmen uncovered the crypt and discovered Dymphna's tomb, made of a shining white stone of a kind found only hundreds of miles away. The townspeople considered it a miracle: God had chosen to honor Dymphna with this sign of care and protection. Reports of healings at the site began to circulate—in particular, healings of people said to be insane—and the site became a pilgrimage center. In 1247 Dymphna was canonized as the patron saint of the mentally ill. A makeshift hospital was built, and in 1349 work began on a new church, the Church of St. Dymphna, which became a pilgrimage center. Families brought their mentally ill loved ones to the sanctuary for healing and, in some cases, left them, still ill, at the church. A "sickroom" was added to the church in 1480, a small two-story brick structure that jutted at right angles off one side of the church. This facility cared for the most ill among the pilgrims and became a point of entry for patients into the evolving community care system. In time, however, the hospital and sickroom proved inadequate for the numbers of people who were drawn to Geel in search of healing.

At first, church members participated in caring for these souls by bringing them food and clothing. As the numbers of pilgrims swelled, the local priest decided to take the matter a step further. He asked the townspeople to take patients into their homes and make them members of the family. In the economy of the Middle Ages, where everyone played a role in ensuring survival, this meant that the new member of the household also helped out with the cooking and cleaning, or by working in the fields or the shop. Thus was family care born in Geel: healing and recovery provided by what we would call foster families.

Early on, it was recognized that there were patients so disturbed that families could not manage their care. For these cases, the sickroom and the hospital, staffed by an order of Sisters, continued to provide places of shelter and healing. Family care became the main thrust of the Geel approach, though; the hospice facilities came to support the efforts of the community based in the homes of private citizens.

Such practices were unheard of. Elsewhere throughout Europe, people who behaved strangely were not considered sick; they were believed to be possessed by demons. They were locked away in prisons or banished from their homes and communities. In some places they were burned to death. Not so in Geel. Records show that, as early as 1245, citizens had been taking these suffering souls into their homes and caring for them in a spirit of compassion and dignity.

I first heard about Geel from Bud Fichtler, a mental health professional in our Seattle congregation. Bud had heard about Geel's history and thought that there were still some families taking mental patients into their homes there. I pictured a handful of neighbors keeping up an old practice in some small block or two. In 1992, I visited Geel.

"Do you know the legend?" my guide in Geel, the local family care program coordinator, asked me at our first meeting.

I did not, and so, over coffee and pastries, she told me the story of the Irish princess who became the patron saint of the community. She also filled me in on the story since the discovery of Saint Dymphna's tomb and confirmed that the tradition of citizens' taking the mentally ill into their homes continued through the centuries. When Napoleon I ruled the region in the early nineteenth century, he ordered that all mentally ill persons be committed to asylums. The people of Geel resisted, refusing to hand over their "family" members to be sent to an anonymous institution. Throughout a history of imperial wars, occupation, famine, and plague, even through the two world wars of the twentieth century and down into today's era of modern medicine, Geel has maintained the tradition of family care, seeking the maximum well-being of all in the community.

A large board on the wall of a conference room listed the names of seven hundred families in the town who among them were hosting more than eight hundred individuals in their homes. This was certainly more than the handful of caring neighbors I had expected. Above the board was one of Geel's symbols, a clock with no hands.

"This means that when you have a home, it is yours for as long as you need it," said my guide. Family care can be a lifelong welcome and support.

What has emerged in Geel over the centuries is an integrated network of care. Eventually, the improvised hospital and sickroom were replaced by a central psychiatric hospital. The gifts of science and research have become part of the community's healing fabric; up-to-date treatments, including the complete range of today's neuroleptic, antidepressant, and mood-stabilizing medications, are a part of patient care. The church, which had organized and supported the program, eventually transferred the operation of the family care service to the municipality. In 1948 the psychiatric center and the family care program were integrated into Belgium's national network of care, with financial support from the Ministry of Public Health budget. But to this day, it is the community, the families of Geel in their life together, who form the heart and soul of the care program.

Today, the town of Geel is organized into five large neighborhoods. Every neighborhood has a mental health house. Each house is home base for a five-person team that supports the family care residents and their host families in that neighborhood. Each team includes a psychiatrist, a psychologist, a nurse, a social worker, and a family practice physician. The nurse visits each person in care, at home, at least once a month. As much as possible, treatment is provided as part of the course of ordinary life.

The mental health houses also serve as neighborhood community centers for patients, who come together for a wide range of activities. There is, for example, a weekly swimming program at the neighborhood pool, a practice dating back to the days of communal baths before families had indoor plumbing. The care team joins in the swim, finding this an excellent occasion to observe their patients informally and inquire after their health.

In the home, family care residents have a room, share meals, and are encouraged to take part in the life and tasks of the house. In one home that I visited, an older woman was living with a young single mother and her two children. The older woman experienced some continuing degree of fear if she had to go more than a block away on her own, but in the presence and security of her care family, she felt safe and functioned in many ways as any live-in grandmother might.

Family care residents participate in the work and service of the community, too. Several economic niches have become their special province. One is a small printing operation that produces almost all of the announcements used by Geel citizens to share the news of births, weddings, and other important family events. Another is a book-bindery program that specializes in repairing old and treasured books and Bibles, and making nicely bound collections of family

histories and records. The psychiatric center has a floor devoted to oc-
cupational programs; the staff helps patients identify their particular
gifts and learn how to apply them productively.

Patients come into the family care program through the central
psychiatric hospital, which is located in the middle of town, just a
few blocks from the Church of St. Dymphna and the original hospice.
There, patients are carefully diagnosed and stabilized before they begin a placement process. The first step in this carefully designed program is to introduce the patient to the prospective care family; this
takes place in the hospital. Next comes a visit to the family's home,
then a meal shared with the family, then an overnight stay, and then
a weekend stay. The process allows time to become acquainted, to
make adjustments, to ease into a life together. As the placement proceeds, the neighborhood care team deepens its involvement. In Geel,
where this process has been repeated thousands of times over hundreds of years, the work of the Spirit is not hurried.

Everyone on the neighborhood team spends a half day in the hospital, assisting their colleagues and getting to know individuals in
the inpatient setting. Family care patients have already met members
of their outpatient team in the hospital, helping with the inpatient
program in various capacities. Moreover, each member of the inpatient staff spends a half day in one of the neighborhood mental health
houses helping with the outpatient program.

Even after the primary responsibility for a patient shifts to the
family and neighborhood care team, hospital and neighborhood care
continue to be well integrated. Inpatient and outpatient staff meet to
coordinate the details of the discharge and placement process, and
they consider possible therapeutic admissions from the neighborhood to the hospital in cases where a patient may need more intensive care. The hospital is also available in times of family crisis; for
example, if members of a care family need to travel out of town to attend a relative's funeral, the patient can stay in the hospital during
that time. Such "well stays" are usually brief, and they offer an added
benefit: patients see the hospital not from the perspective of an acute

episode of suffering, but in a state of health; this helps them gain a greater appreciation for the healing efforts of inpatient care.

In Geel, the care is holistic, multifaceted, and proactive. It is collaborative in the truest, mutual sense. No one presumes to be all-knowing or all-powerful. Collaboration is evident in every aspect of the program.

From the legend of a family tragedy, a mentally ill king and his daughter, was born a caring community that endures to this day. Geel is a daily miracle of compassion, a continuing story of promise and potential. The clock without hands symbolizes not only a home for as long one has need, but also a timeless persistence of care, steadfastly provided over the centuries.

Legends and symbols are means by which we express and communicate our faith. We tell stories and share unique events to help us illuminate our existence. We use the simplicity of symbols to convey the truths that are most important to us. Our spiritual lives are rich with ancient tellings and signs of God's presence and the movement of the Spirit in the world.

Stories and symbols give form to our faith. Creation stories speak to us of the "why" and horizon of our existence, and point us through the natural world toward the sacred in all that comes into being. Stories of spiritual journeys awaken us to the Holy in our lives. The lives and teachings of Abraham and Sarah, Moses, the Old Testament prophets, Jesus, and all who have carried faith forward down through the ages illuminate our human path. Parables and poetry, wisdom and revelations blend into an ever-unfolding testimony that shapes our life together and provides frame and structure for our faith.

Through story, the Spirit shapes us as communities. Myth, legend, history, parable, drama: story in its many expressions helps create and sustain religious life. Stories are at the heart of a people's soul; stories give substance to our shared spiritual identity.

But there is much that our forebears in faith did not know or understand; there is much that we have learned that is not included in our ancient scriptures. Mental illness is an example. Mental illness as such is not a subject of discussion in the Bible. We have descriptions of people who display symptoms of a mental disorder, such as the man of the Gerasene miracle, but their stories are told from the limited scientific understanding of the era. There was very little medical knowledge of the brain in biblical times, no field of psychiatry, no neuroscience. In the thousand and more years following the accounts of Jesus's ministry, we find only a few abbreviated histories and mentions of mental illness and its care, ranging from the brutal to scattered examples of more enlightened and supportive approaches.

The story of Geel gives voice and visibility to the subject of mental illness as part of the larger story of faith. The legend tells us that those who suffer brain disorders, and their families, are not forgotten. The caring practices of Geel bear witness to the activity of the Spirit at work over the millennia to shape and sustain a community of faith that includes our neighbors who are mentally ill. The clock without hands suggests that the Spirit's care for us is timeless; it is a work of centuries, an eternal care. And the evolution of the Geel model from an improvised, church-centered response to an urgent need, to a sophisticated, twenty-first-century alliance between highly trained practitioners and ordinary citizens, suggests that healing is not found exclusively in either the sacred portals of the church or the health provider's office, but in the fullness of community life. Geel invites us to consider how the Spirit works not just in individual lives and personal relationships of care, but also in our life together as neighbors, as citizens of towns, as nations, and as a world.

The Geel model has inspired community-based care programs elsewhere. One example is Lierneux, a rural town with a regional psychiatric hospital and outpatients living in farming villages and hamlets across the area. Here, some two hundred families in a more sparsely populated region of French-speaking Belgium provide homes for family care residents. The program, now nearly two centuries running, was adapted from the Geel model to fit the local setting and culture. The biggest difference between the two programs has to do with the rural setting of Lierneux. Its quieter, agricultural environment is reminiscent of Geel at an earlier time.

The ethos, however, is the same. Lierneux, like Geel, centers on the role of family care in healing and integrating patients into the community. My conversations with members of the staff pointed out two qualities that make the family care model so effective in the healing process. The first has to do, simply, with the number of stable individuals in the family relative to the person in recovery; in the family care setting, a patient is surrounded by other healthy people. In contrast, patients living in a congregate-care, group setting outnumber the staff. Those living on the street have even less access to care and few, if any, supportive relationships. Family care nested in neighborhoods of hospitality and understanding provides a rich environment of health.

In the community-wide fabric of acceptance and encouragement, we see the second quality that makes family care so effective: family care normalizes the illness experience. A patient is welcomed into a home with illness as a given; it is a part of who he or she is. The purpose of family care is to build and nurture a new but, in many ways, quite ordinary life for patients around and beyond their illness—not denying, suppressing, or replacing the illness, but making it part of a fresh, ongoing journey.

This normalization has a larger social dimension. The care families and residents are part of a network of service and support that is recognized and valued in the wider community. In Geel, family care homes exist in all five neighborhoods; in Lierneux, they are scattered throughout the little town and the surrounding region. Residents accompany their family members to the store, the library, the café, the movies, the park; they are a part of the daily flow of life into a variety of work and service settings. Each resident has an intimate cadre of knowledgeable intermediaries and advocates helping to address stigma and stereotypes, fear, ignorance, and prejudice.

Family and neighborhood become allies in healing and care. They form a support system in patients' journey toward wellness, and they can also serve as an early response system when patients show signs of relapse or increased symptoms.

The value of family care is demonstrated in yet another place I visited, Bobigny, a suburb of Paris. The Bobigny program focuses especially on young adults with serious and persistent schizophrenia. At the time of my visit, twenty-four families in the community were participating in the project.

Several things are key to the Bobigny approach. First, the professional team cares not just for the patient, but for the whole family involved in the care program. As the program psychiatrist put it, "Family care does not work without care for the family."

Accordingly, the professional team meets regularly with patients and with the families as a whole, attending to questions and concerns of the foster parents and siblings. Whenever possible, these meetings include the patients' natural family as well.

"We begin with a few threads," the psychiatrist explained, "sometimes quite slender and easily broken. But we keep hold as best we can, and we keep weaving, weaving, weaving, creating a stronger and stronger cloth of relationships. It becomes a beautiful tapestry, telling a beautiful story."

I had gone to Europe hoping to find ideas and existing practices yielding wisdom that I could take home and apply to my work in the United States. What I discovered, in the first place, is that in Belgium, there is a national network of hospitals and community clinics covering the country. The Ministry of Health provides the basic budget for mental health services. Regional governments organize the local programs, including education, outpatient care, and hospitals. The actual service providers are a mix of nonprofit and public entities. Ninety percent of the psychiatric hospitals and 80 percent of the clinics have in fact been founded by church groups. As Geel and Lierneux suggest, there is creativity and vitality at the local level.

The mental healthcare network contrasts dramatically with the mental health system in the United States, where attempts to establish an effective, nationwide care network several decades ago foundered. In 1963 Congress passed the Community Mental Health Act, which was strongly endorsed by President Kennedy, who had a sister who had been institutionalized. This act called for the creation of a community mental health center for every two hundred thousand people across the country. Each center was to be a beacon of education and prevention for its community, with a twenty-four-hour walk-in clinic and an inpatient floor where individuals with acute symptoms could get immediate and appropriate care. In addition, each center would have an outpatient program offering care for recovery and support over the long term. The centers were to be run by community boards comprising local citizens who would organize care and treatment in the ways best suited to local conditions. This public community mental health network was to be built up as the state hospitals began to downsize and close.

State hospitals did downsize, and many closed. Sadly, however, fewer than one-fourth of the community centers were ever constructed, and not many offered the full range of anticipated services. Organizing and funding public mental healthcare in this country has remained largely a state responsibility, delegated to local or regional government. The quality and kind of care available differ widely from state to state. Alongside the public mental health facilities, there exists a separate, private set of hospitals, clinics, and psychiatry practices, paid for by private insurance plans. As we saw with Karl, it can be excruciatingly difficult to find and qualify for care within this fragmented patchwork of services.

The nationwide network of mental health services in Belgium is part of the broader system of universal healthcare delivery. Everyone is a part of the same system, patients and doctors alike. There is a private sector, and some doctors do have private psychiatric practices, but my impression is that it is small compared with the overall system. One psychiatrist with whom I spoke told me he had an office that he used one afternoon a week to see three or four private patients.

"We know what good practice is," he said to me. "We want high-quality care for everyone. I don't just *work* at my hospital and clinic. It is my family's hospital and clinic, too, where we go if we need care."

And where do the churches fit into the picture? In Geel, I asked one of the family care chaplains what kind of special programs the churches had for patients in the family care program. He looked at me quizzically, and I described a few of the things we did in Seattle: spiritual support groups, Bible study opportunities, companionship ministries. My colleague from Geel said they didn't have any special programs; the family care residents did what everyone else did in the churches—they sang in the choir, helped usher, participated in various small groups.

"They are," my colleague said, "part of the congregation, like everyone else."

Part of the congregation, like everyone else. The most striking thing I took home with me from this tour was a sense that the programs which truly work exist within a certain community attitude, a spiritual milieu that accepts as normal—so normal that it is unquestioned—a common responsibility for the well-being of all.

"It is an honor to be a family care provider," a chaplain in the Geel program told me. "My family has done it for generations. We had two family care residents living with us when I was growing up."

Staff members were interested in my work in Seattle, but they were appalled when I told them about the numbers of homeless, mentally ill people to be found on our streets. That's criminal, they said. In Belgium, homelessness is against the law. This does not mean that police go about rounding up the homeless and tossing them in prison; it means homelessness is not allowed to exist. Local officials are responsible for making sure there is long-term care and housing for all citizens. Local and regional officials can be held liable if there are people who do not have care or housing.

And indeed, I did not see people on the streets ill-clothed and showing signs of an untreated mental illness; I didn't see them in Geel or Ghent or any other Belgian town I visited.

Referring to some of the situations I had experienced in my years on the street—cases like Jerry, for example, who had frequently gotten out of control, or Walter or Ally—I asked one of my hosts what happened when individuals became so ill or agitated that they might warrant involuntary treatment.

"We would say that they are having a bad day," my host said.

"What do you mean?" I said.

"Here in Geel, it would be very rare for a person to become as ill as what you describe. People do have bad days. They become sicker. Symptoms appear or reappear. But for us, the emphasis is on providing care as soon as possible. When people begin to have bad days, we act. We don't wait until someone is at their worst before starting care."

"We have a long ways to go," I said, thinking about how many individuals in America can't get help until they are in deep crisis.

"Ah," said my host. "Remember, we have been working on this in our community for seven hundred years."

I saw his point. In Geel, the movement of the Spirit is a long-term phenomenon. The love of God in the world is made real through many generations of caring human activity. The fullness of faith is experienced not individually, but in common, through people in relationship with one another. The Geel experience bears out the truth that our healing, our wholeness, our *souls* take shape in the context of community. We are healthy only in company with one another. Geel speaks to the question, Can *I* truly be well if my sister or brother remains abandoned, lost, or sick? In Geel the answer is that our salvation is social. The Spirit moves to heal and help us all, not one by one, but in company with each other.

In Geel and Lierneux, people facing the journey with mental illness are seen not as burdens, but as sisters and brothers, each with a contribution to make, a calling to share with others. The cities have organized themselves not to separate out those who experience extraordinary episodes of brain activity, but to ensure that they are actively welcomed and included, thereby enriching the soul of the community.

I had gone to Europe because my work among the homeless mentally ill had raised questions in my mind about the inadequacies of healthcare in my own community. I was searching for ideas and hoping to find better practices. In Geel and Lierneux and Bobigny, I began to understand the importance of a strong, community-wide approach to mental health, well supported at every level of society.

In Geel, everybody knows the legend. The story of Saint Dymphna is so powerful that it has inspired a way of life that has lasted for more than seven hundred years. Begun during an era when belief in miracles was high, the practice of family care in fact embodies that central message of the Christian Gospels. Jesus's life and ministry find their expression in the love and care shown by the citizens of Geel to the most vulnerable and suffering souls in their midst. In Geel, the great feast is shared daily.

9

HOME, HEALING, AND WHOLENESS

Tonight there are nine chairs around the dining room table. Selindra and Abby have prepared the meal. As we gather, food arrives from the kitchen: platters of roasted chicken, a casserole of tofu in a curry sauce, bowls of fruit and vegetable salads, a loaf of bread, pitchers of juice and water, and a box of soy milk. Laughter and greetings connect us. As the last seat is taken, a brief quiet settles over the room.

Abby begins the ritual. "I'm just grateful for the sun today."

Folks smile. It's Seattle, and the past week was full of gray "oyster days" when the sun stayed hidden behind a low cloud cover.

Others around the table speak.

"I had a good appointment this morning—everything went okay. I'm grateful for that."

"I'm grateful that we got to go to the ball game last night."

"I'm glad James is here."

"The food," says Bethsa, who speaks very little English.

"I'm grateful for caterpillars," says Josie.

Folks laugh.

"I'm serious," Josie says. "Caterpillars are warm and fuzzy and a sign of spring, and they are going to turn into something beautiful. I saw one today."

Next to Josie, Bethsa looks puzzled. Josie holds her fingers out, measuring about an inch.

"Caterpillar. It's like a furry worm. It turns into a butterfly," Josie explains.

Bethsa still doesn't understand. Josie pantomimes a worm, then a cocoon, then a butterfly. More smiles around the table. Abby takes a pen and draws a caterpillar on her paper napkin, and next to it a butterfly. She points to the caterpillar, then cups her hands together to form a cocoon. She opens her hands as if releasing the butterfly. Bethsa smiles, finally, and nods her head.

The group waits as Solomon considers his gratitude for the day. He has just moved into the community after being on the streets and a recent stay in the hospital.

"This house," he says.

The circle of gratitude comes to me.

"I'm grateful for each of you who make this house a home." I glance up to the bright red ceiling and white box beams of the dining room and say, "I'm also grateful to Carl, who helped design this house with his love for warm colors and light." Carl is the architect who oversaw the remodeling of the house, and he personally painted the ceiling.

There is a pause.

"Let's eat," says Abby.

Four of the people at the table are residents, living at the house for three to six months as they convalesce and begin their recovery from an acute episode of mental illness. Four others are volunteer companions who give a year of service by living at the house. I am a guest.

We are in Plymouth House, an eight-bedroom home located a short bus ride from the Harborview Medical Center on a street with a mixture of apartments and single-family houses. It is an old neighborhood, and many of the buildings, like Plymouth House, have been there since early in the last century. At one end of the block, however, is a newer structure, an apartment building for seniors; at the other end is a small city park where a diverse community, a little United Nations of neighbors, gathers to splash about in the wading pool, play basketball, enjoy a picnic, or just soak up the sun when it's out.

You can easily recognize Plymouth House because it has a red door and a hammock on the front porch. Inside, your eyes immediately pick up the stairway, which Carl painted a bright blue. Through a doorway to the right is the living room, furnished with comfortable chairs and couches on a woven oriental rug. A set of double doors leads to the dining room, where the red ceiling echoes the color of the front door. The kitchen contains two refrigerators and plenty of nourishing food. On the back side of this floor are two bedrooms, a bathroom, and a small office. Upstairs are six more bedrooms and two baths. From every room there are glimpses of the distant mountains. In the basement is a family room, some storage space, laundry facilities, and a small area reserved for meditation and meetings. The front yard is filled with plants; the space in back is divided into a patio and a garden area. The driveway is shared with the next-door neighbor.

Plymouth House has been in operation since 2001, and it represents a small but important success story in community care. But it did not spring into being overnight.

Upon my return from Geel in 1992, I was excited to share with others what I had seen and learned. I dreamed of recruiting ten or twelve families who would serve as the basis of a small family care program in Seattle, supported by one of our mental health centers and a group of congregations. Perhaps, I thought, we could build a model of family care in one neighborhood, which could eventually spread to other areas.

But there were some difficult questions: Who would recruit, screen, and support the families? What kind of training would the families need? Would they have to be licensed? What were the liability issues? How would this be paid for? What had started so simply in thirteenth-century Geel seemed much more difficult to begin in late-twentieth-century Seattle.

The movement of the Spirit, though, seldom proceeds by following a formula or imposing a rigid, one-size-fits-all pattern. The challenge of ministry is not met just by repeating what others have done, however inspired and compelling their models; every ministry must grow from its own soil, in response to the human needs of the particular time and place. In Geel, the Spirit has been moving through the centuries, creating a deeply rooted culture of compassion; that Spirit is at work in every community, awakening our capacity for compassion and inspiring us to build healing communities that go beyond rescuing individuals in crisis, to proactively foster health and well-being in our own settings.

The Mental Health Chaplaincy, my home base in Seattle, had been working closely with Plymouth Church, a United Church of Christ congregation in the heart of the city. In the early 1960s, the church had helped found the First Avenue Service Center, a day drop-in program for folks on the street. Over the next two decades, downtown Seattle lost twenty-five thousand units of low-cost housing to high-rise commercial development, and people were now sleeping in increasing numbers around the church. In 1980, the church, heeding a Geel-like call from Pastor David Colwell, created the Plymouth Housing Group (PHG), a long-term effort to save and create low-income housing. PHG soon began adding buildings at a rate of one nearly every two years.

During this same period, state mental hospitals began to downsize and close. The first wave of patients was discharged to nursing homes, but increasingly, those who had once been housed in hospitals now found themselves on the streets. The population in Washington state hospitals went from six thousand patients whose stays averaged twenty-five years to a current population of less than sixteen hundred with an average stay of six months. Plymouth, like many churches, discovered a new and growing group of people coming in the door: individuals struggling with symptoms of mental illness, often without medication, disconnected from care and treatment, confused and despondent.

In 1987 the Chaplaincy offered the first companionship-training course for laypeople at Plymouth, and a Sunday-morning companion team was formed to welcome people who came to services in distress. Community companion teams were also formed to serve during the week in Plymouth Housing buildings, shelters, and drop-in centers. Thus, Plymouth companions developed a firsthand body of experience within a growing continuum of care for homeless persons in downtown Seattle.

Progress had been made, but there was one glaring gap: homeless people were receiving treatment and care in the hospital, but just as they began to be stabilized, they were discharged back to the streets with little or no follow-up. They had to fall in line behind others on the waiting lists for subsidized housing. They left the hospital with two weeks of medication and an appointment at a community mental health center, where they might eventually get help with their illness and assistance in finding housing.

The change from the supportive environment of the hospital was dramatic. On the inpatient units the ratio of staff to patients was one to one, with twenty-four-hour care. In a shelter, a person might be one of several hundred in the care of three or four staff members, sleeping in a large, open space inches away from the next person. Hospital social workers estimated that they were discharging more than one thousand persons a year from the psychiatric units to the streets or shelters without any well-established connection to outpatient care.

The need was clear. What could we do?

In a moment of serendipity, I spotted a battered old book on a table at St. Mark's Cathedral, where the cathedral's library volunteers were giving away copies to clear out the shelves. I read the word "Healing" on the cover, but the rest of the title was too stained to be legible. I thumbed through a few pages and read about a network of houses adjacent to hospitals in rural areas of South Africa. The Anglican Church had created these houses as convalescent centers where people who had come from a great distance could live for a time after their release from the hospital while they grew strong enough to make the trek back to their home villages. The Church had recognized a need. People were well enough to leave the hospital, but still too ill to make it back into the community on their own. The "houses of healing," as they were called, provided a communal support center for patients during the early stages of their recovery.

I stuck the book in my backpack and read it through as soon as I had a chance. I began to picture such a house available to patients on the mental health units who would otherwise have to make the difficult and uncertain trek on the streets of Seattle. Why couldn't we marry the "house of healing" idea with the practice of family care—a house of healing in which residents coming from the hospital would be embraced by a family of support and encouragement?

The Chaplaincy board agreed to convene a small working group, which included a representative from Plymouth Church, to explore the idea. Our immediate vision was to establish a house of healing somewhere near Harborview, the county-owned public hospital, to welcome residents directly from the psychiatric units for a stay of three to four months while they convalesced and secured permanent housing. We hoped to duplicate the hospital's one-to-one ratio of caregivers to patients, or even exceed that level—as in Geel, where a family of two, three, or more persons provided support to each person in recovery. We aimed at providing a round-the-clock presence so that fragile souls would have someone who would be present, no matter what the time of day—a factor that would be helpful to the residents of the house and reassuring to the surrounding community.

In Seattle, city housing ordinances allow eight unrelated adults to live together in a single-family home without requiring special zoning permits and licenses. This legal fact prompted us to focus on a house community composed of four companions and four residents. Our rough plan called for prospective residents to be enrolled in a community mental health program before leaving the hospital, so that when they arrived at the house, provisions for outpatient psychiatric treatment and case management services would already be in place.

We presented the idea to Plymouth Church, which in 2000 was undergoing a discernment process to develop several new major mission projects. Building on its history of care with those on the streets, the congregation decided to make one of its new projects a mental health ministry that would include an educational effort, support for individuals facing mental illness and their families, the creation of a house of healing, and advocacy for an effective community mental health system.

I helped staff a team that began planning for the Plymouth House of Healing, or Plymouth House, as it came to be known. We consulted with a number of people who had experience with running group homes for various populations—people with physical or developmental disabilities, women in transition from situations of domestic violence—and providers of housing for persons in recovery from mental illness. We got some particularly good advice from David Hilfiker, a physician who had helped start Joseph's House in Washington, D.C., a hospice for homeless men with terminal illnesses. He stressed the importance of each resident playing an active role in the life of the house, "to do whatever they can to contribute," he explained. "For someone who is terribly sick and has little energy, it may be something quite small, but we want to recognize that each person's presence among us is a gift."

We also consulted with people who themselves had been homeless, who had been in the hospital, and who had made the journey to stability. Terri, the erstwhile guardian of the cathedral steps, was an early enthusiast who had not only suggestions but something tangible to offer: the round dining-room table at which she, Father Ryan, and I sat for the housing blessing when she first moved into her apartment—the table she called her "ecumenical" table.

"You can have it for the house," she said, "a table for everyone."

Terry's table sat only four, though I'm sure she would have tried to fit five thousand around it if she could.

As we continued to collect ideas, we gradually laid the framework for life in the house. We explored with our partners at Harborview how the discharge process worked and how we could meet with patients who might be interested in coming to the house. We strove to minimize the barriers and details that made it hard to get someone enrolled in outpatient care. And we also got to work on the house itself. We needed a property located on a bus line to the hospital, and near enough that outpatient staff could easily make home visits. We needed to figure out how to acquire the property—and, of course, how to pay for it, both the price of the property and the year-to-year costs of maintaining it and running the program.

After a near miss or two as housing prices crept up, we found a house that met our criteria. By the time the Plymouth congregation voted its final approval of the project, an "angel" had stepped forward to purchase the house and hold it in trust until we could eventually raise the funds necessary for taking title to it ourselves. At the congregational meeting, David Regnier, presenting the proposal, noted that the Spirit had certainly been active, encouraging us to the point of having the house itself in hand.

"It seems good to the Spirit," he suggested. "How does it seem to us?" The congregation voted unanimously to proceed.

In all, more than three hundred people were involved in the planning, purchase, renovation, and furnishing of the house. The energy they invested is literally in the walls, the floors, and every piece and part of the house. Each contribution is an expression of the Spirit's care and encouragement.

After a careful search, we hired a house manager with the right combination of managerial skills, experience in running a household, warmth, compassion, patience, and levelheadedness. And then we recruited our first four volunteer companions, who included an attorney in the midst of a career change, a young man who had interned with the Chaplaincy, a young woman recently graduated from college, and a retired public health nurse.

With the companions in place, the residents began to arrive. I visited the house one day and discovered that one of the first residents was Norm, a man I had worked with on the streets. Norm had been deeply distraught. He hadn't been eating, and for months he hadn't spoken a single word to anybody. As I walked in, Norm was sitting in the living room, listening to the conversation of several others and waiting for dinner. When I entered, he looked up shyly and said, "Hi, Craig." Deep healing was beginning to occur, restoration within and reconnection with others.

A second resident had been hospitalized five times during the past year. A third arrived with an undiagnosed addiction, which became quickly apparent in the context of life at the house. A fourth resident was a recent immigrant to this country, presenting the companions with the challenge that they not only appreciate the extraordinary experience of a mental illness, but have sensitivity for someone whose beliefs and customs were quite different from their own.

On a scale of 1 to 10 in terms of difficulty and challenge, our original intention was to start with patients who were closer to 1 on the scale and gradually work our way up to persons with more complex and challenging illness experiences. As our first four residents settled in, I asked our liaison at the mental health center where we were on that scale.

"Closer to 10 than 1," she said.

Some patients came to the house still experiencing symptoms of depression. They moved tentatively and were uncommunicative; they kept to their rooms, reluctant to come to dinner. Their unresponsiveness was disconcerting; their remoteness and lack of interaction left a void. Others arrived with lingering symptoms of bipolar disorder, their thoughts still racing, their bodies overflowing with energy. The rush of their ideas and opinions made it hard to get a word in edgewise, and they sometimes came across as rude, insensitive, arrogant, and intrusive in ways that were overwhelming for the companions and other residents. Still others suffered occasional recurrences of delusions or hallucinations—voices heard or things seen: events disturbing to both the residents and the companions. Several residents who wrestled with drug and alcohol issues relapsed.

How do you hold the emptiness of those who are depressed? How do you respond when someone talks about suicide? How do you manage, and at the same time care for, those who have only partially returned from the euphoria and grandiosity of a manic episode? How do you set limits, honor personal boundaries, and secure respect for your own needs? How do you comfort and reason with someone for whom the line between reality and illness is cloudy? What do you do with the few worn and frayed threads of selfhood and human connection a person may offer? These are a few of the issues that have confronted Plymouth House from its inception.

On the street and in the house, the usual structures of healing—the architecture of the clinic and office, the framework of appointments and scheduled hours of care, the regimens of diagnosis and treatment—are not readily available. Companions and residents meet each other in ordinary time throughout the day, and in space that belongs to all. They share the bathroom and break bread together at the same table, shaping personhood and human community mutually in countless moments of awkwardness, immediacy, and authenticity.

I have come to respect and admire how intimately the companions at the house assert and establish themselves with care. Every encounter is an engagement with the healing process, an embracing of both the remaining effects of illness and the potential for wellness and growth. Hour after hour, from the dawning light to the evening's last "good night," companions give and receive, not in heroic perfection, but in honest humanness.

The house community discovered early on that each individual is far more than just a set of symptoms, a diagnosis, or even a patient in the process of treatment. Each resident has his or her own history—as did each companion—a complex experience of shaping and interpreting themselves and their world. The task of seeking the truth, coming to a common understanding of health and well-being, and building a meaningful life together is ongoing and constant.

What is most challenging is not the brain disorder itself—the biochemical imbalances or the symptoms and behaviors directly issuing from mental illness. Understanding and companioning the residents' psychological, social, and spiritual struggles is the fuller, and more difficult, task. It is hard for the companions to hear and absorb residents' accounts of homelessness, the estrangement they have encountered, and their deep woundedness. Companions come to an understanding of the illness process and a realization that healing in the brain takes time; they become conscious of the house as a home not only for convalescence, but for personal renewal and growth. Companionship is not simply about supporting treatment and care; it is also about the recovery of worth and dignity, a meaningful selfhood, and the realization of potential and possibility. Companions listen as residents share feelings long blocked, hurts rarely expressed, dreams lost, and hopes voiced, perhaps for the very first time. Each resident coming into the house is like a new birth, asking the house family to gather afresh and grow yet again. These were among the challenges faced by the first companions and the first residents of Plymouth House, a community that is, to this day, still very much in process.

I think of Plymouth House as a seedling rooted in groundwork prepared by a host of forebears, brought to life by the dedication of imaginative colleagues and fostered by a people faithfully engaged at the fragile edges of society. Along the way, all who participated in the project experienced the impetus of the Spirit in our collective lives, moving among us in many small moments of personal investment, countless decisions to be open to the stranger, hours of careful meditation and reflection, and in our willingness to question, dialogue, and decide faithfully, each step of the way.

The process of spiritual change, growth, and social action rests in many small moments of preparation and encouragement. Plymouth House emerged from months of discernment, growing wisdom, and consensus building. The process begins at the most personal level—the "Samaritan" level—when we are touched by another's helplessness, vulnerability, and need for tenderness. The Spirit is to be found first and foremost where gentleness is required: in the crib, at the bedside, in the raising of a child, in our intimacy with one another, and on the street with those who are most fragile and wounded.

The Spirit is at work not just within us each, but also *in our life together at every level of human organization.* Just as the Spirit moves in the most minute moments within our bodies, it moves in the unfolding of family in its various forms, the creation of neighborhood, the organization of community, and the formation of society. The Spirit seeks our well-being, not just in terms of health and moral character, but also in terms of public witness and social justice. The Spirit has concern for our common life—for the ways we treat one another as persons, manage care and human services, provide housing, keep order, use the resources of the planet, steward our environment, divine our callings, and give expression to our varied gifts and abilities.

The Spirit is present when we come together to share our grief and concern, and hold our experience of suffering and struggle in common. The Spirit is present as we seek direction and open ourselves to service. The Spirit offers illumination and encouragement as we begin to organize and make real our hopes and dreams. The same Spirit that provided guidance in the planting of Plymouth House is ever available to all who suffer, all who stop by the side of the wounded, and all who would be builders and keepers of an inn-filled world where no soul is left out or left behind.

As new residents arrive at Plymouth House, they are welcomed by the volunteer house companions. Each person has his or her own room, furnished with bed, dresser, and desk. Quilts, handmade by a group in the church, add color and warmth to each room.

Each afternoon, the companion "at home" prepares dinner, inviting others to share in the preparations. Monday through Friday, the house community shares the evening meal, beginning with the ritual expression of gratitude. Laughter and conversation punctuate the hour together. Residents and companions both are quieter at the beginning of their stay, but they usually gather self-confidence as the weeks go by. People are who they are, and they share themselves with the group as they are able. Each evening is another opportunity to be with others, to offer and observe, to venture and try, to be heard and recognized and valued.

A resident named David said he had never before in his life sat down for a regular meal with others. "This is the first time I can remember having the same people with me every day at the same time."

David had touched on a basic healing practice of the house. There is always someone at home, someone present to receive and hold, to represent structure and framework, to explore both limits and possibilities, to offer empathy, to serve as a model and mirror, someone present to listen and share the journey.

It is a primary covenant of the community that the residents and companions nurture each other and support healing and growth, and the evening meal is a staple of that covenant, a daily act of commitment to being present with one another. It isn't always easy. Residents sometimes forget the time, arrive late, or are tempted to go off somewhere with friends. The companions, too, wrestle with the commitment. It is hard to say no to invitations or forgo opportunities that might lure them away once or twice, or "just on Tuesdays for the next few weeks." Such tugs from the world outside can pull at the slowly weaving fabric of community, causing the life of the house to unravel a bit. Six o'clock is not a magic hour. The hands reaching this moment act as a sign not of the passing of time, but of a desire to *make time for each other* as a priority in the life of the house. Always it is a process.

Companions create a schedule ensuring that at least one of them is present twenty-four hours a day, 365 days a year. In addition to the four live-in companions, the house manager and a small roster of part-time volunteers help out. One companion is available throughout the night should a resident need support.

Christina, in her illness, heard voices, and when she came to Plymouth House she was still hearing voices. She was traumatized and always on her guard. She spoke in whispers and spent a lot of time hiding in her bed.

"I'm trying to protect what little there is left of me," she said one afternoon.

A companion at the house started a small spiritual support group that met around readings from the *Gentle Bible,* a little book of verses adapted from the Bible. Christina attended the gatherings, sitting quietly as several verses from the *Gentle Bible* were read by first one person and then another. Each person was asked to hold on to whatever word or phrase spoke to them and then share the word with others.

From the readings on the first night she attended, Christina centered on the word "courage."

"Courage," she said. "That's the word I want to hold."

There is a prayer that asks, "Speak to me the word I need to hear." In the house of healing, the community seeks to embody a core language of care and understanding, healing and hope. Christina experienced moments of great fearfulness, but in those moments others in the house were available to speak words of assurance. They came to her side and accepted her as a person. They did not turn away from her fear but, rather, shared their own frailty and found, together, strength for recovery and growth.

After she left Plymouth House, Christina joined a church choir. I ran into her one day during the fellowship hour after a service and asked her if there had been anything that was particularly helpful to her during her stay at the house.

"Lots of things," she said. She thought for a moment and then laughed. "One of the companions told me I was brave. I had never thought of myself that way." She paused again for a moment, standing with her hands on her hips, and then added, "The house didn't make me brave. They saw that I was brave, and I am."

Courage is a vital quality in recovery, and Christina is right: the house doesn't make its residents brave. However, the house provides an environment in which every person's capacity for courage has an opportunity to develop. Among friends who care and offer their support, resiliency sprouts and strength increases.

Like Christina, Denny found new reservoirs of courage while at Plymouth House. Denny was a former truck driver who started using drugs to help him stay awake on long hauls. His life became increasingly chaotic, with swings of mood that went from deep depression into manic highs. He lost his job and housing and landed on the streets. It was many years before he finally received hospital treatment, and then, upon his release, lived in Plymouth House through the first months of his recuperation.

After leaving the house, Denny volunteered to speak at a church gathering we had organized, to celebrate the first anniversary of the opening of Plymouth House. To our surprise, more than eighty people showed up. We had to bring in extra chairs and stretch the food to feed everyone. Standing up in front of an audience is intimidating for a great many people. For Denny it was an enormous challenge— far more than many of us had realized. In addition to his bipolar disorder and his struggle with drugs, Denny told the gathering that he also experienced agoraphobia, a debilitating anxiety about being out in public places in the midst of strangers. He looked out on a crowd bigger than any of us expected and kept speaking nevertheless.

"I was on the streets for a lot of years," he told us, "and for a lot of my life it has been hard for me to be around people. I didn't want to come to the house, but I didn't have anywhere else to go. I would never have made it in a shelter, I couldn't have gone in the door. But I also knew I couldn't make it on the streets anymore."

Denny recounted how at first he stayed in his room most of the time. He didn't talk at dinner. But slowly he began to feel at home. Nobody pushed him.

"The fact that I'm up here today in this room, speaking to you all, is something I never thought I could do. It's still not easy. But I wanted to do this, to show you how the house helps people. Thank you."

The house welcomes a remarkable spectrum of individuals. While residents share the common ground of a struggle with serious mental illness, each has had their own particular experience. It is the gift of the house both to recognize the common elements of the journey and to celebrate the uniqueness in each resident. The residents arrive with their own personal and social backgrounds, creating a wide diversity of ages and cultures within the house family. Thirty percent are immigrants or refugees, some arriving at Plymouth House speaking very little English. Companions also come at varying stages in their lives, from many parts of the United States as well as from other countries.

Each person in the house has a story, and all benefit from the warm and accepting atmosphere where everyone's life story is received with care. In sharing their stories, residents and companions alike come to know better who they are as persons. One person's painful experiences become the shared concerns of the community. People discover strengths they didn't know they had, and receive others' support to develop those strengths. Response and feedback help an individual to see better how he or she affects others and how the world of others sees and shapes them. Every day, residents and companions live a new and common story, a story that is increasingly filled with health, hope, and possibility.

At the most profound level of each person's story emerges the narrative of the soul: one's spiritual identity, one's full richness as a person, one's wholeness. The life of Plymouth House cares for the soul and nurtures the movement of the Spirit in each person's journey. Whatever the religious culture each person brings, it is honored and encouraged as a helpful element in healing. Plymouth House is a multifaith house of healing. Its foundation lies within Christian tradition, but residents and companions have brought to their stay the spiritual gifts of Judaism, Buddhism, Islam, and Native American traditions. The house has been a home for believers, seekers, and skeptics, all contributing to a rich spiritual exploration.

The basement meditation room, where members of the community can come to reflect quietly or share in spiritual practice together, will sometimes reflect this diversity, as, for example, when a group gathers to study the Christian Bible, blessed by the presence of a delicate floral offering left by a Buddhist member of the house community.

In the common rooms on the main floor, people share their religious experiences and spiritual concerns as part of their general and wide-ranging conversations. Companions and residents alike understand that this time of convalescence can be a time of spiritual vulnerability in which sensitivity and openness are paramount. Each person's point of view is respected. The house is a way station, a place where a variety of pilgrims come together. All are aware that they are together for a particular time and purpose, and then they will move on. The house encourages each person to find a long term community of faith supportive of their particular pilgrimage.

Each person's room is a private sanctuary where individuals keep and treasure what is most supportive and dear to their soul. A tattered scrap of prayer, carefully wrapped in saran and tucked in an old water-stained wallet, has sustained Jimmy through his worst time on the streets and his most acute episodes in the hospital. A Bible rests in the top drawer of Elizabeth's dresser. She takes it out and brushes her fingers across the letters of her name inscribed on the front in gold, connecting with her past and feeling her worth in the present.

From each room of the house one sees a different view. Each room looks out on one of the different mountains that surround Seattle. In a way, this symbolizes the spiritual horizon shared by all, as well as the unique viewpoint of each resident. Each has his or her personal moments of revelation and truth; each brings his or her particular faith journey to share and celebrate. Each makes a unique contribution of soul to the community, and all are enriched by one another.

The same tone of openness and mutual respect guides the house in matters of internal governance and conflict resolution. The house has rules, but they are not absolute or immutable. New situations come up, and a way forward must be found. When a problem or question arises, the community engages in a process of discerning a resolution together, seeking consensus through a practice borrowed from the Quakers. The community sits down. Each person has their say and is heard without argument or judgment. A direction or decision is proposed. Again, each person speaks in an effort to seek wisdom. It is a process that honors the gifts of each individual; the assumption is that truth comes of the Spirit, working not just in one single mind but in the collective wisdom of the community.

The community's deliberative approach to consensus building is meant to ensure that the voice of the timid is equal to that of the confident. Dissenters are valued for their differing viewpoints, for they help the group see issues from another angle, often helping to reveal what otherwise might be missed.

All of this contributes to a healing atmosphere. Residents come to the house, perhaps acutely aware of being "abnormal" and alone in their illness world, but in the house of healing, it is *normal* to be "abnormal," to have had extraordinary experiences. Every day the grief and suffering of illness are acknowledged. In the house, the illness experience is surrounded by health; as in the homes of Geel, residents find support for the new life that is emerging within themselves. The mental health team provides treatment that helps reduce the symptoms and force of the disorder; the house shapes together a home life that nurtures each person's new and growing being.

There is an ancient Greek word that characterizes the life of Plymouth House: *liturgeia,* which literally means the "work of the people." The derivative English word "liturgy" has come to mean not so much the work of the people, but the forms and flow of worship; thus, for many, spirituality has come to mean the way we sing, pray, preach, serve Communion, or baptize. At Plymouth House, spirituality has to do with the daily work of being people, of living together in community. The liturgy of the house—its spiritual life—is made up of many small, unseen moments of care and encouragement. Every meal is a Communion. Any conversation may become a moment of renewal and reconciliation, any act a sacrament of touch and salvation.

More broadly speaking, the house demonstrates the healing power of community. The healing power of community is not just the sum of many individual parts and acts. Each member of a community— any community—brings gifts to the life of the group and becomes a channel for the common good. The community together creates the environment in which wounds are healed and individuals can build wholeness.

Plymouth House does not stand alone. It is part of a neighborhood and a wider community. It was our hope from the beginning that the house of healing would be a center of service and a resource for the neighborhood. We envisioned neighbors joining in the life of the house, coming to dinner, stopping by to visit—in other words, becoming acquainted with the residents and companions in ways that would dissolve the stigma and myths that surround mental illness. We knew that in every neighborhood there are individuals and families with their own mental health struggles, and we hoped that the house could serve as a small outpost where someone might get information, encouragement, or a connection to help.

We were aware that we risked running into a NIMBY ("Not in my backyard") response. We met with neighbors at community organization meetings and also talked with them informally as the house was remodeled. People raised concerns about their own safety and the behavior of residents. We emphasized that it was important that this effort work for everyone. We intended to do our part to support the well-being of the neighborhood. We believed that maximizing the spirit of healing in the house called us to work also for helping to create a peaceable and supportive neighborhood, a wider community of people who understand and care. In short, we sought to become, as fully as possible, the "community" in "community mental health."

Our colleagues at the Harborview Medical Center have been thoughtful and responsive partners. From the beginning, we have enjoyed an ongoing dialogue, collaborative planning, and excellent co operation from them. We have successfully navigated the potentially difficult waters to bring a faith-based organization and a publicly funded hospital together to meet a glaring human need. We have developed a model that is replicable, a framework of partnership from which other communities, congregations, and mental health centers can draw helpful lessons. We hope houses of healing will come into being elsewhere, and we trust that the spirit of healing evident in our effort will inspire others to reach out according to the needs and conditions of their own community.

In addition to its healing function, Plymouth House has become a small center of community resources, education, and advocacy.

Realizing that the amount and variety of permanent housing is still very limited, the Plymouth House board has responded to opportunities to develop two shared-living houses and a pilot companioned-apartment-building program. Another, larger companioned apartment building is in planning. The project's growth has led to a new name, Plymouth Healing Communities, to reflect the expansion of the effort.

The companions themselves have become an important gift from Plymouth House to the wider community. Each companion who spends a year at the house leaves with a deeper appreciation of the nature and impact of mental illness in a person's life. And all carry the story of their experience with them on their continuing journey, to share and live out with others. As I write this, two former companions are in medical school, and several have gone into social services and counseling. Imagine a physician who has spent a year living with patients, seeing life from the "illness" point of view. Imagine social workers who have participated in the daily details of convalescence and recovery, and who have gotten to know, at an intimate level, the struggle with mental illness and what is involved in making a healing journey.

Plymouth House is the result of many small miracles, and a vivid example of the gentle activity of the Spirit among us. As much as we may wish for the "Damascus road" moment—the dramatic intervention, the revolutionary change, the immediate implementation of our hopes and dreams—the Spirit most often works incrementally. The Spirit leads us on a path of many steps. It is not so much in the destination, but in the movement from day to day, that we discover what makes for healing and salvation.

The family care program in Geel began when a pastor and his community stopped to care for the neighbor lost and alone in their doorway. Plymouth House is rooted in the life of a congregation that has consistently reached out to the neighbor who is homeless and, with no inn available, has created sanctuaries of care and support. When ordinary people stop to care and follow the logic of compassion to its fullest expression, they can change the character of a community. The seedling efforts of a few radically hospitable citizens can begin to transform a neighborhood. Multiplying these efforts locally and creating a society that supports ready and widespread care are the concrete tasks of realizing the Spirit's highest aim.

The Good Samaritan stopped by the wounded man at the side of the road and gave him first aid. He did what he could and then took the man to an inn. There he arranged with others to help in the healing work, for as long as was necessary.

In a sermon at Riverside Church in New York City, the Reverend Dr. Martin Luther King Jr. said, "We are called to play the Good Samaritan on life's roadside; but that will be only an initial act. One day we must come to see that the whole Jericho road must be transformed so that men and women will not be constantly beaten and robbed as they make their journey on life's highway."

Like Dr. King, I believe that we are called to offer more than individual first aid. We are called to share in work that shapes healing neighborhoods. When there is no inn, we are called to create places of welcome and care. When our systems and institutions and policies and programs as a society fall short of supporting health and well-being, we are called to work together to make our community more just and humane, in concrete ways. Plymouth House is an example of our calling to be "social Samaritans"—not merely to heal individuals, but to shape a world that supports the well-being of all. It is an example of social action, a mission that entails not just picking up the broken pieces, but helping to shape a society that is proactive in caring for those most fragile in our midst.

In the spiritual tradition from which I come, the call to social action, the call to caring for the condition of the world, has been a compelling element since the beginning of time. In the book of Genesis, we are called to be stewards of the earth and become part of a covenant of care for one another. The mandate of our life is not individual success or achievement. We are called to be a people who actively share and do right by one another. We are invited into a covenant marked especially by tenderness for those who have the least and need the most.

In the book of Judith, one of the narratives of the history of the Israelites, we read: "Your strength does not lie in numbers, nor your might in violent men; since you are the God of the humble, the help of the oppressed, the support of the weak, the refuge of the forsaken, the savior of the despairing" (Jth. 9:11). God's care and strength are made real in the world in the neighborhoods we create with each other.

The Psalmist wrote, "God gives the lonely a home to live in" (Ps. 68:6). But the homes must be built by our hands and the doors opened by our love for one another.

The tenderness of God does not wait for suffering to unfold before acting. God knows our frailty as persons and seeks through the power of love to create among us the foundations and institutions, the paths and the policies, that make for health. Through the Spirit, God seeks to establish a covenant with us to create together a world at peace, flowing with justice and abundant in life, especially for those most vulnerable among us: the child, the alone and isolated, the bereaved, those who suffer, and those who are ill.

These are the "least" among us to whom Jesus referred in the last verses of the twenty-fifth chapter of the Gospel according to Matthew. These "least" are the first concern of the Spirit, souls who have the highest priority in the heart of God.

"Seek ye first the kingdom of God," said Jesus (Matt. 6:33). What is this "kingdom," this world born of the Spirit? It is a world not of armies, but of shepherds. It is a world not of palaces and thrones, but of birthing new life in humble, ordinary inns. It is a world in which love and gentleness, mercy and grace, courage and great care are the foundations of neighborhood and the basic practices of life among us.

10

CARING FOR THE SOUL
OF THE WORLD

In the spring of 2000, I was invited to Bosnia to help in an effort to rebuild the country's community mental health system. For almost a decade, the lands of the former Federal Republic of Yugoslavia had been torn apart by warfare in Croatia, Serbia, Bosnia-Hercegovina, and Kosovo. More than one hundred thousand people died, either in combat or through violent measures that came to be known as "ethnic cleansing." More than two million became refugees. Modern weaponry reduced city neighborhoods to rubble, obliterated roads and bridges, and destroyed social service networks. The United Nations, NATO, and the United States intervened to end the fighting and establish peace.

During the war, Bosnian hospitals lost a staggering 90 percent of their psychiatric beds. Over the previous decades, a network of community mental health centers had been developed, but that, too, fell victim to the conflict. Training and educational facilities were lost. The fabric of community, neighborhood, and family support for individuals facing mental illness was shredded as fighting swept through the region and entire communities were slaughtered or forced to flee.

More than four years after the end of the Bosnian war, I visited with people there who had finally received funding to rebuild their mental healthcare network. Three pilot teams had been selected to train together and provide leadership in different parts of the country. I met first with the team operating in Banja Luka, a predominantly Serbian city; then with the team in Zenica, a predominantly Muslim city; and finally in Sarajevo, where the population was mixed.

The basic question we addressed was how to involve ordinary citizens in local care efforts. There simply were not enough profession als to do all that was needed. Postwar reconstruction had been slow, and basic infrastructure—such necessities as electricity, water, sewer, schools, general hospitals and clinics—still had not been rebuilt, and these needs had priority. The mental healthcare teams knew they had to be creative, both in mobilizing the citizenry to help and in providing services to people where they were, that is, in their homes, on the streets, and in makeshift clinics. I came not as an expert, but as a fellow pilgrim on the quest to create communities of care in a world too violent.

Rea Maglajlić, the program director, had asked me to speak as part of the opening of the training program in each of the three pilot cities.

"It is important," she said, "that we know we are not alone in this work."

With each team, I described the companionship-training model we use in Seattle and talked about our outreach on the streets, in shelters, and in day centers, working wherever someone was in need. I talked about the hundreds of thousands of people with mental illness wandering America's streets and languishing in our jails. I said I had come to learn, share, and participate in a movement to create healing neighborhoods. The challenge, as I saw it, was twofold: developing a fabric of care in our communities that would include and support the most vulnerable among us, and developing sensitivity and compassion as the basic foundations of our life together.

At the end of the first day in Banja Luka, the team members and I adjourned to a small café for coffee and a light evening meal. We sat out on a patio, overlooking a park on a warm early summer evening.

During a lull in the conversation, a psychiatrist on the team whom I'll call Dr. Đurić asked if he might speak with me alone for a few minutes. We moved to one corner of the patio and stood near a railing above the stream passing through the park.

"There is something I must say to you," he said. "You and I both know that it is not healthy to keep deep feelings of hurt and resentment inside. It does not help to pretend that everything is okay when it is not."

I agreed, with a touch of uneasiness about where this conversation was heading.

Dr. Đurić was a soft-spoken, earnest man in his midfifties, with wavy, graying hair. He was a Serb, originally from Bosnia, but he had gone to Belgrade, the capital of Serbia, to help out in a clinic there during the height of the Kosovo war. In an attempt to stop the escalating violence between the militarily dominant Serbian security forces and the Albanian Kosovars, NATO had intervened with air strikes against the Serbs, meant to force the government of Slobodan Milošević to make peace. At first the strikes concentrated on military targets, but eventually NATO's bombers turned toward Belgrade itself, hitting civilian neighborhoods and causing a great deal of suffering.

Dr. Đurić looked me in the eye and said, "One of your American planes bombed my clinic in Belgrade and destroyed it."

I was stunned. For the moment, I had nothing to say.

"I kept thinking about that this afternoon when you were speaking," the doctor said. "Your plane bombed my clinic. I'm still angry. Seeing you, an American, has brought that up. But I am also angry at my government. We have been badly led."

I recovered from my shock enough to convey my sense of sadness. I told the doctor that I saw in my own country the effects of militarism, the lack of adequate public funding for health and welfare, and, in particular, the neglect of the homeless.

"The cost of that bomber," I said, "would build many clinics in your country and mine. The cost of that one bomb would buy the medicine our people need."

Dr. Đurić continued. "You and I must do more than pick up the pieces. We must work to stop the violence. Already too many need our help in your country and mine—and all over the world. We must learn together how to care for souls, and for the soul of the world."

*   *   *

In the morning, there was no water in the city. Repairs were still being made to the pumping/treatment plant and the lines of supply. The team continued to meet, carefully sharing emergency stores. For me, however, it was time to go on to my next stop, Zenica, a day's drive in Rea's car. On the way there, the road gave out at a river marking the edge of the Serbian-dominated sector of Bosnia. The bridge had been blown up. We forded the river at a shallow crossing, picked up the road again a few hundred meters farther on, and reached our destination in time to get a night's rest before meeting with the Zenica team the next day.

In a large room, a dozen of us sat in a circle. The team was a mix of Bosnian Serbs, Muslims, and Roman Catholics. Introductions went around the circle, and I began with a brief description of my work in the States with those whose refuge was the streets. Then I told the group of my conversation with the Serbian psychiatrist in Banja Luka and invited them to share their stories of the war.

A social worker spoke up. "You are the first person who has asked us that. Thank you. We've been so busy caring for others that we have not had time to tell our own stories."

They spoke of their own losses and grief, and the challenges of providing care under conditions of siege. One team member observed that, in some ways, the war had drawn people closer, as all had to pull together.

A Muslim woman I'll call Melika told an extraordinary story. She was a psychiatric nurse, but in the war she worked in whatever capacity she was needed. One day she was tending to an old man, a Roman Catholic, who was dying. He asked Melika to get a priest to perform the last rites for him. The hospital was in a section of the city controlled by a Serbian militia, whose men were almost all of Eastern Orthodox Christian background. To reach the nearest Roman Catholic church required passing through to the edge of the Serbian sector and then crossing a sector occupied by a militia made up mostly of Muslim troops. Both crossing points were fraught with danger, but Melika made her way through to the Catholic church and the priest agreed to go back with her.

"The priest wore his cassock, and I had on my nurse's pin," Melika said. "We walked in the open and hoped nobody would shoot at us. Nobody did. When guards stopped us, we said we were going to care for a dying old man. We were aware of the danger, but for the priest and me, no one was the enemy. I wanted my patient to know in his last hours that he had the blessing of his God."

Tears began to roll down Melika's cheeks. "We can hold in our hands healing or guns," she said. "I choose healing."

We all glanced at each other in silence, sharing our sadness and our common hope. After a moment, a single voice began a soft, almost imperceptible chant. It was music I had rarely heard, the sonorous tones of the Orthodox liturgy. As the chant died away, a second quiet voice sang a Kyrie Eleison (Lord, have mercy), a response from the Latin liturgy of the Roman Catholic Church. Melika murmured a prayer from the Islamic tradition. The room grew silent again as we felt the Spirit of love and healing in our midst.

Next, Rea and I journeyed to Sarajevo, the capital and heart of Bosnia, a multicultural community with some seven hundred thousand inhabitants today. Before we met with the team there, Rea took me on a tour. Many buildings were damaged or destroyed. Rea pointed out places where snipers on the hills had shot citizens as they dashed across open spaces, heading for home or safety. In the center of the city, we walked to the Catholic cathedral, then a few blocks farther to the Serbian Orthodox cathedral, then a block or two more to the Jewish synagogue, and finally to the lovely, sixteenth-century Gazi Husrev-beg mosque. Rea pointed out that the houses of worship for these four great traditions had stood in peace together in the heart of the city for nearly five hundred years.

We met with a Franciscan monk, one of a small group of brothers devoted to furthering and deepening the multifaith life of Sarajevo. He gave me a recording of music made by the Sarajevo Peace Choir, made up of singers from the different faith communities in the city. We talked about what might be done to create a multifaith training of laity to serve as companions in their congregations and communities.

"What is at the heart of companionship?" he asked. "What is the core of the training?"

"Hospitality," I said. "Welcoming the stranger. Creating safe space. Breaking bread together. Listening with one another for the movement of the Spirit and the presence of love."

The monk smiled. "Hospitality," he said, "is a basic practice in every religious tradition. We have that always in common."

The night before my departure, Rea and I walked again through the streets of Sarajevo and up a path leading to a view over the town. She thanked me for coming. It was important, she said, to hear that we in America were also struggling to build communities that bring people together and include those who are most isolated.

"This is the groundwork for peace," she said.

We stood in silence for a moment, looking down at the city lights.

Then she said, "I wanted to share with you the special soul of this little country. We must not let this war destroy the work of the Spirit here. What we are doing together now is an antidote to violence. We are trying to be neighbors again, as we were for centuries before, trying to learn again how to care for each other. This is Sarajevo's tradition, Bosnia's purpose: the real treasure we have to share with the world."

Throughout the former Yugoslavia, the work of repair and reconciliation goes forward. Hospitals are being rebuilt and clinics are reopening. New generations of healers and caregivers are being trained and educated. In Sarajevo, congregations meet in cathedral, mosque, and synagogue. Still neighbors, they are finding in the depth of their faith shared wellsprings of care, mutual respect, energy, encouragement, and hope.

I began my career in the ministry during our country's struggle for civil rights and the war in Vietnam. Seventeen years later, the Mental Health Chaplaincy was born in a world still in the grip of the Cold War. At the end of the last century, a meeting of the World Trade Organization brought thousands of demonstrators and the rage of global poverty to the streets of Seattle. We live our day-to-day lives amid forces that seem impersonal and beyond our control.

Yet what counts is what you and I, and our Bosnian sisters and brothers, do at the most local level. What is most true and creative in the world are the ordinary human beings who give of themselves in acts of care and kindness, day in and day out, across the globe. Mothers are giving birth. Parents are raising children. Crops are planted and harvested, water drawn, cups filled, bread baked. Animals are tended, boards hewn, bricks made, shelter built. Commerce and trade proceed. Schools and clinics are created, roads constructed. Learning and wisdom, culture, law, and tradition are shaped. Families and tribes, villages and neighborhoods, grow. All these are gifts of the Spirit and expressions of the tenderness of God.

It is with immeasurable compassion that God holds all that is injured in the world, taking up each wound, bearing with us each loss, enduring with us our suffering. God's infinite gentleness outlasts the most persistent powers of illness and destructiveness. God's transforming power constantly renews and restores the world at every level of life, beginning in the minutest moments of existence. The Spirit, constantly moving, offers health and well-being, even and especially in the most hidden, unlikely, and unpromising places.

Think again about the Christmas story, through which we celebrate the presence of God come into the world in an obscure birth, in the life of a child who grows to lead not an army or institution, but a local movement of reconciliation and love, healing, and growth. We are invited to be part of that movement, the Spirit work of caring for one another and the soul of the world.

To be sure, we come to many of life's responsibilities unprepared. We are challenged to learn as we go. We ask ourselves, "Who am I to help? What can I really do?"

I recall how little my wife, Barb, and I knew of parenting at the time our daughter Kelsey was born. We had taken a childbirth class, and it helped us immensely through the moments in which Kelsey came into the world. But little were we prepared for what was to come, including the simple grief of having Kelsey for several days in an incubator under bili lights to correct a blood condition that affects some newborns.

Once we got her home, I had much to learn about the requirements of fatherhood. My parents came to visit us, and I was proud to hold Kelsey in my lap at dinner. She was quiet and cuddly at first, but then grew agitated. She clearly needed a diaper change. I excused myself to take care of this task—it was the first time for me—and returned to the table with Kelsey bundled up neatly in a fresh sleeper. I was inwardly proud of my newly acquired changing skill—until Barb pointed out that I had only done half the job, forgetting to put on a new diaper.

All of us are called to care for one another, but even for the most basic tasks we may have little experience and must learn with each other's support.

As with parenting, we may find ourselves unprepared for the responsibilities of neighborhood and citizenship. But it is in growing our families and weaving the fabric of our communities that we discover our capacities for caring and develop the practices that are at the foundation of a healthy life and a peaceable world.

Health and peace begin each day, in every community, with how we treat one another. How we act on the larger stage of human affairs is rooted in the ways we have practiced at home and on the sidewalks and street corners of our communities. We cannot ignore our sister or brother's suffering, we cannot turn away from the stranger in need before us and expect that we will somehow have the knowledge and skills we need to create well-being and lasting security on the national or global level. A peaceful world grows only on the foundation of compassionate community, laid down as generations of humans cultivate and spread the practices of companionship, the art of hospitality, the gift of listening, and the capacity to walk with one another—and especially the stranger—toward a shared well-being.

We lay the foundations of a peaceful and just world community by community, by reaching out to our most vulnerable sisters and brothers. Learning to care for the stranger on our own street gives us the basic tools and understanding we need to engage those we fear in the larger world. If we are afraid of our troubled neighbor, if we steel ourselves to pass by and ignore the suffering of our fellow human beings on the sidewalk, if we distance ourselves from their need and protect ourselves by segregating and quarantining them in the least desirable parts of town, we give support to the societal attitudes and policies that have left them without home and care. If we cannot learn to live in harmony and practice compassion with those of our own neighbors who are "different" from us, how can we expect to live in peace with those from other cultures, around the globe, whom we find difficult to understand?

In Banja Luka, I listened to my brother health worker express his pain at seeing his place of care and service destroyed by a distant warrior, an airman in the sky who took his orders from his military superiors, who, in turn, took their orders from a command post carrying out a mission determined by strategists thousands of miles away. I can believe that none of those who commanded and carried out the bombing mission knew they were destroying a place of refuge and healing. So who is responsible?

We are. As individuals, as communities, as congregations, and as a human family, we are responsible for one another. As citizens, we have sufficient power and hold collective responsibility for orienting our priorities as a people and our policies as a nation toward healing. This stance has deep roots in the message of the biblical prophets, and its most practical incarnation in Jesus's ministry. The work of healing, the task of building inclusive and caring community, the living of a daily life of love for the stranger and the outcast—this is the heart of our calling as human beings.

It is here that I wish to plead a special calling for those of us who have experienced the devastating symptoms of mental illness. Sterling Hayden could testify to the potential for terror in the world.

Driven by schizophrenia to the church courtyard for protection, Sterling lived in the presence of an indescribable evil. Johnny M., a man whom I met in an alley downtown, adds his witness. No battle in heaven or on earth could match the apocalyptic experience Johnny described to me as he sat shaking in his alley, convinced that bodies were falling about him in an interstellar Armageddon. Millions of people around the world suffer similarly in gulags of mental disorder, prisoners of a war from which only armies of love and care can rescue them. Let us turn our energies to engage these real and devastating battles in every community. Here with our family members, our friends, and our neighbors is the first and most nearby front against war, suffering, and terror.

Now, at the beginning of the twenty-first century, terror preoccupies our collective consciousness. Fear of terrorist attacks has replaced fear of nuclear holocaust. The threat of uncontrollable forces at work in our world colors our discussions of politics, foreign policy, and national defense; it impinges upon our basic freedoms and disturbs our national priorities. Our fear has driven us into a lengthy and difficult war. Yet we understand so little about the power and place of fear in our lives.

When we begin to understand fear and terror on the individual level, we will be better able to understand how fear and terror, multiplied by thousands and millions of human beings, predispose the collective mind to defensiveness and violence. When we begin to understand despair and hopelessness in the life of one suffering person, we will become better able to understand how despair and hopelessness multiplied by thousands and millions of people driven by poverty and exploitation can build into acts of desperation and destruction.

When we begin to understand how vulnerable the human brain can be to hallucination and confusion, we will be better able to understand how susceptible we and our leaders can be to false reports, manipulated evidence, inadequate intelligence, hidden motives, uncritically examined ideology, and propaganda. When we realize how our brains may slip into disorder and confusion, we become more cautious about the claims of authority and truth we make. We know that our behavior can come from unexamined and obscure processes within us. We know that our brains and minds, our emotions and feelings, our thoughts and faiths are complex—and, in the end, frail —gifts.

We all have much to learn by engaging the journey with mental illness and listening to those who suffer its impact on their lives. It is not simply that we must forge ahead with all possible research to identify the causes and alleviate the suffering; we should, by all means, do that. But more: God calls us to understand that these disorders are an expression of our complex nature as human beings, aspects of our wholeness as persons.

The treatment team is called to diagnose and respond to the extraordinary symptoms that arise in us when our brains, perceptions, feelings, thoughts, and relationships become profoundly disturbed. All of us are called—family and friends, neighbors, and citizens— to understand and companion, to offer maximum support for the human self in repair and recovery. We are called to develop our life together in community to ensure the fullest well-being of us all. And we are invited, in all these endeavors, to nurture each person's sacred identity as an individual and as a member of our diverse human family.

We begin caring for the soul of the world by caring for the souls of our neighbors, for each life that touches ours.

As we serve with those who are most wounded, we find ourselves drawing upon the deepest wellsprings of our faith, our taproots into the life of the Spirit. We do not all have the same words, the same journey, the same story; that isn't necessary. Indeed, to insist that all must see and believe in the same way is to limit the sacred, diminish our experience of the Holy, and block the full power of healing and reconciliation in the world. The human brain does not come with a label saying Baptist or Catholic, Orthodox or Reformed, Sunni or

Shiite, Buddhist or Hindu; and these labels, which we inherit from our ancestors or adopt in the course of our life journeys, do not set any of us off as having superior insight.

Out of the experiences of suffering and struggle together, by accompanying one another in illness and through trauma, we find ourselves walking, as the prophet put it, "humbly with [our] God" (Mic. 6:8). We know it is not this particular activity or that special phraseology which makes for deliverance, salvation, or the restoration of our souls. Deep healing is a spiritual grace, proceeding from a source of care and a word of tenderness, far more powerful—and yet more gentle—than our human language can adequately convey.

Deep healing is where peacemaking begins. Humbly walking with our God—and our neighbor—is the first step. We lay the groundwork when we mobilize our fellow citizens to understand the sufferings of the mind and invest themselves personally in the practices of healing. The structure starts to take shape as we work to reorient local and national priorities in every land toward policies that support caring community as a fundamental goal. As we build healing community locally and globally, we build into the world the DNA, the patterns, the stored wisdom and basic practices, that make for peace and well-being.

11

WORDS ARE MEDICINE, TOO

At ten o'clock in the morning, a man entered the Cathedral of St. James, found his way into the sacristy, and dressed himself in the robes of a priest. From there, he strode into the great worship space and up the three short steps to the altar in the center of the sanctuary. There he stood, as if celebrating the Mass, bathed in light from a clear, glass dome above. A handful of people sat in the nave meditating, or knelt in side chapels, praying.

The sacristan, an assistant to the priests and a safekeeper of the cathedral, quietly approached the man at the altar.

"What are you doing?" the sacristan asked.

The man replied, "I am the pope. Where else would I celebrate the Mass in Seattle but in the cathedral?"

The sacristan politely asked the man to come away from the altar and return the vestments to the sacristy.

"You're welcome to pray or meditate if you wish and, of course, to attend the service," the sacristan said. "The next will be at noon."

"You don't think I'm the pope?"

"No," said the sacristan.

The man returned the vestments to the sacristy and took his leave.

Later that day, another staff member found the man asleep in the guest room of the rectory and again asked him what he was doing.

"I'm the pope," the man said. "Where else would I rest but in the rectory of the cathedral?"

The staff member said, "You don't look like the pope, my friend."

"You don't think I'm the pope?"

"No," the staff member said. "The pope is in Rome."

The staff member asked the man to gather his belongings and invited him downstairs to wait in a room next to the rectory's front door. He promised the man that someone would come who could help him. The call came to me.

When I arrived at the rectory, the stranger looked me over and said, with exasperation, "These people don't think I'm the pope. Do you think I'm the pope?"

He stood, tired and ill at ease. His clothes were worn, and his eyes moved constantly, checking out the room. He held his hands palms out in front of his chest as if to push away anything that came too near. His face showed the frustration of arguing with people who were forever questioning his identity and challenging his beliefs. Please, he seemed to be saying, this is real for me; this is what I am right now.

I could see that this was no time for an argument; the man was alone in his illness and estranged from others. I hesitated for a moment and chose my words with care, speaking with a gentle humility.

"I'm a Protestant chaplain and not an expert on the papacy," I said. "How about this: You are a human being and I am a human being, and we can start there."

"Okay," he said.

I sought simply to acknowledge our most basic identities and give voice to the common ground between us. The man accepted me as a fellow human being who accepted him in the reality of his illness self. The most helpful care I could immediately offer was an understanding that, whatever else was in play between us, we stood essentially as equals. A few simple, dignifying words of introduction and concern got us started on the road toward healing.

"Words are medicine, too."

That's what Tom, a young physician trained in psychiatry and neurology, said when I asked him how those of us who are not doctors could help a person struggling with mental illness. I had invited

Tom to meet with a companionship-training group early in the life of the Mental Health Chaplaincy. Tom outlined for us what science and medicine were uncovering about the biology and biochemistry of illnesses such as depression, bipolar disorder, schizophrenia, anxiety, and trauma. He described how he went about making a diagnosis and considered the medication to prescribe. My question got him talking about the importance of language and communication.

Tom explained that when we speak, waves are set in motion in the air between us and our listener. Those sound waves are gathered in through the ear and pass to the eardrum. As the eardrum vibrates, sound is transformed into biochemical activity, a new wave of energy, which passes into the brain along neural pathways to a complex set of centers governing sensation and emotion, memory, thought, imagination, and action. Our words, like medicine, become an influence on how the brain functions.

"Words can harm," Tom said, "just as the wrong medicine can harm. But words can also help heal."

Even the smallest utterance is an encouragement and an invitation to respond. Our words open intricate channels of relationship. Each time we speak, our words are alive with energy. Every word that passes our lips, every phrase and sentence we utter, has power. The words you share with me touch my brain, affect my mind, and help shape my soul. Your sentences and gestures, the tone of your voice, the language you choose—all carry the potential for healing and growth.

The words we speak begin forming as soon as we come into the presence of another. I recall, for example, a man standing in a downtown doorway one morning with a newspaper folded under one arm. He caught my eye while I was still half a block away. He smiled a little and nodded when a passerby spoke to him, but mostly he stood and stared blankly out at the world. I had seen the man for several days in the same doorway, newspaper under his arm, as if stuck in this spot. On the third morning I didn't just say hello and walk by, but stopped for a moment after greeting him.

"Hi," he said back.

"How's it going?" I said.

"Okay."

"Anything I can do to help? It can be tough out here."

"No, thanks. I'm okay."

"Okay if I say hello again when I come by?"

"Yes," he said, and then went silent.

We repeated this minimal conversation for the next several days, speaking only a few sentences back and forth.

One rainy morning, I found him soaked.

"I'm headed to the shelter," I said. "It's warm there. You can dry out, maybe get some extra clothes."

"Okay," he said.

At the shelter, Mindy, the receptionist, told the man she would be happy to enroll him in the shelter program and asked if he would answer a few questions for the registration card. He glanced back and forth at us, held his hands out, and struggled to speak. Nothing came out. He shook his head. The few sentences we exchanged on our way to the shelter had exhausted his capacity for conversation.

I turned to Mindy. "Can we just call him 'John' for now, show him around, and take it slowly from there?"

Mindy agreed.

Again, a few words were the best John could do. Mindy called a floor counselor over to help this new, and now silent, client settle in. I said goodbye and promised to stop in the next morning.

The following day, John was sitting on the floor, his back to the wall. I knew we had only a small treasury of words to share with each other, and so I waited for a while before speaking, considering how to start in a way that invited John to tell me as much as he could about his experience before he shut down.

"I've noticed that we can say a few words to each other, and then you're quiet. Can you help me understand what happens?"

"The words go out of my head," he said.

"I see you've got a paper again today."

His newspaper was open to the Help Wanted classifieds.

"I get up and find a paper. I see a job. I circle the ad. Then my mind goes blank."

"Is that beginning to happen now?"

"Yes," he said.

"I'd really like you to meet a friend of mine. He's a doctor who has some understanding of this kind of thing."

John nodded.

The next day I introduced him to a psychiatrist who was doing part of his residency training at the shelter. It was a slow process. John did his best to answer questions. In the first session, he was able to share his name and a bit of basic personal information. In the second session, we learned that John had graduated from a local high school and had worked on a construction crew. He began to forget things and came to believe he was just stupid. The other workers made fun of him, and he was let go. In the third session, the doctor asked John how he would get from the shelter to his old neighborhood.

"I would go down to the street. I would look for a bus."

John fell silent.

The doctor asked gently, "What next?"

"Gone," said John, holding out his empty hands and shaking his head sadly.

The doctor diagnosed John's condition as a form of schizophrenia and prescribed medication that gradually restored his ability to hold onto ideas, carry on conversations, make plans, and follow through. John found housing and left the shelter. In time, he returned to his family and took a job.

John's healing began with a basic language of care: gestures of recognition and respect, words of greeting and encouragement, a simple vocabulary of acceptance and mercy.

The language of care starts with our senses. Before I speak to you or you call out to me, our bodies are aware of each other's presence. My eyes take in the sight of your being, the clothes you wear, the wound in your arm, the burden you carry, the tiredness in your eyes.

My ears hear the sounds of your life: your feet approaching, your rasping cough, the nervous tapping of your hand, the sigh you release. My nose picks up the smell of the garbage-filled alley where we stand, the faint odor of urine in the doorway you've been sleeping in. In the heat of the day, my mouth is dry, like yours, and I can feel your thirst. My feet hit the same hard concrete that you walk on. I can feel the roughness of your hand, the brush of your breath.

You, too, have the gift of sensation; you, too, form an impression of me. I walk slowly, approach gently. I wear soft khaki pants and a pair of well-worn, never-polished shoes. I have on a serviceable beige jacket and a comfortable old Irish cap.

Before we ever speak, the Spirit is helping to open the channels between us. What we see and hear evoke a range of emotions in us. This is the work of the Spirit, moving through our senses and touching our hearts, even before a word leaves our lips.

The language of care is greater than the act of speaking. It is a language of sensitivity, patient presence, and gentle approach; a language of concern and mutual respect. It does not depend on our particular roles or the labels the world gives us. Healing words flow from our common humanness, our feel for a person's life condition, and our compassion for someone else's suffering.

When I met the man who thought he was the pope, communication began well before we spoke. A range of relational channels was open to us. I chose to move down the dial, away from the daunting and complex frequencies we use to discuss roles and labels, tuning instead to the most basic wavelengths of human connection and conversation. We affirmed our status as neighbors, fellow inhabitants of the same world, the same city, this same small patch of ground. In this initial moment, the specific definition of our roles was not important. The man in the cathedral was not the pope, but he was no less a child of God than you or I—or the pope, for that matter; the important thing was that two human beings met. In the most basic language of care, in the way we stood with each other, in the words that honored our fundamental worth and dignity, healing began.

At business and social gatherings of all sorts, we introduce ourselves as players of a particular role: I'm a chaplain. I'm a dental hygienist. I'm a landscape gardener. I run a construction company, sell shoes, enter data, clean houses, drive a truck, take tickets at a movie theater, fish, develop software, and so on. In our homes we are parents, mothers and fathers, sons and daughters, siblings. We take comfort from having some defining framework for approaching and engaging others. Our role gives us a specific identity and provides a warrant for being where we are, doing what we are doing, and saying what we are saying.

But whatever our particular role or calling, in the end we walk together and stand on common ground as human beings. We live and breathe, have need of food and shelter, and depend upon one another for nurture and growth. We share this planet. Ultimately, we are all guests passing through this particular time and place. In our humanity, we are equals.

Healing words take shape as we share in the moments of brokenness together, no one of us ultimately above, in front of, more worthy or better than another. Words of care and concern come in our vulnerability to each other, our tenderness with one another.

You will remember Jerry, the man barred from every service center in the city. He and I were walking downtown on a wet winter afternoon, Jerry in one of his irritable moods, when I noticed a young woman huddled in a bus shelter. I stopped for a moment to observe her. Jerry also looked and grew subdued. I took a few steps closer and asked the young woman if she was okay. She glanced up, her face red and raw from wind and tears, and shook her head. She had on a light jacket and flimsy sandals, and sat shivering in the damp Northwest cold. I asked Jerry to wait for a moment.

I knelt down next to the bench on which she was crouched and asked if there was anything I could do to help. Her name was Gillian. She had been asked to leave the apartment where she was sleeping on a couch. She was alone and afraid. She didn't know where to go or what to do.

Jerry was standing close behind me.

"She's cold," he said. "She's scared. We should take her to the center. Get her some coffee, some clothes."

"This is Jerry," I said. "He knows the streets. He's suggesting we go to the First Avenue Service Center, where it's warm and there's food and folks who can help."

Gillian looked up at us and tears welled in her eyes. "I need to see a doctor. I ran out of meds. I'm losing it. The people I was staying with couldn't take it anymore."

I said there was another nearby resource, Angeline's, a center for women, where a nurse was often available.

Gillian's body shook and she began to sob. Jerry looked stricken. I prayed silently that the Spirit's gentleness would hold Gillian and open a door for her. Slowly, her crying subsided. I stood up and she arose. Together, the three of us took the next steps toward her healing, along streets crowded with other people on their way home from work. At Angeline's, simple words of introduction gained a welcome for Gillian. Further words of reassurance and kindness led to her ongoing care and eventual recovery.

One might have been tempted to think that Jerry's own illness rendered him incapable of feeling the pain of another person, that his own troubles overwhelmed his capacity to empathize with others' suffering. But no, Jerry was touched; concern welled up in him as it can in every human being. The constant work of the Spirit is to open and amplify our capacities for sensitivity and compassion, awaken concern, and help us form words of healing and care.

Concern is the Spirit's work within us, mobilizing the energies of tenderness. In the words "she's cold," Jerry expressed what his senses told him about the young woman. In two simple words, "she's scared," Jerry expressed the openness of his heart. In suggesting that we go to the center, he voiced his concern and pointed in the direction of help. Through this rumpled castoff, the Spirit found a channel to articulate healing words. I do not know what Gillian thought of Jerry, or even if she heard him at all, but his voice aided my own.

Moving from the bus shelter, the three of us formed a tentative circle of care, a rudimentary community. Where only moments before a lone soul sat surrounded in silence, heartbroken and cold, a story of renewal was in the rising.

Healing words flow naturally from us in the face of suffering. We introduce ourselves, share our concerns, and begin the journey together. In the rhythm of speech and silence, we offer our presence. At each step of the way, our words help us recognize the course we are on and sign the path ahead.

Think of John in the doorway, his mind going blank, or Gillian at the end of the day, crouched in a bus shelter. It can be daunting to open oneself in such vulnerability to others. Caring conversations are essential to bear a person forward as he or she journeys to each new station on the road to healing.

Words, however, can be poisonous.

"Move along. You can't sit here."

"Get out of the doorway, you're blocking the entry."

Such words as these, spoken to someone like John or Gillian in their distress, only wound further an already troubled soul. Even benign and seemingly appropriate words can be ineffective medicine. We give someone a list of resources. We write down an address. We look up a phone number. We suggest that a person in difficulty go somewhere or see someone. But when the brain is malfunctioning, such encouragements or instructions may be difficult to understand. When someone's feelings, perceptions, or thoughts are deeply disturbed, he or she may not be able to follow even the simplest directions; words of compassion may help, but what the person needs most might be accompaniment—someone to go with him or her and make sure an appointment is kept and care is received. Effective support calls for a language of humility and collaboration. Healing words acknowledge that wholeness is ultimately a shared grace and well-being is communal.

When the psychiatrist Andrew Borland spoke of "healing coming toward us," he expressed how the work of the Spirit forms a crucial part of the recovery process. The language of the Spirit and the vocabulary of faith provide words that help us understand the meaning of such healing. Recovery, well-being, and indeed our wholeness are, in the end, the story of souls, the story of our connectedness to one another at the deepest levels.

One by one, people enter the chapel inside a large downtown church. It is a quiet, circular space with white walls and colorful banners hanging between stained glass windows depicting doves. Chairs ring the room in two circles, and there are pillows on the floor. Candles light the space on this gray December afternoon. The participants have brought small treasures, symbols of help and hope for their journey: a book, a yellow and red scarf, a family photo album, a bell, a violin, a Frisbee, a set of keys. One man has brought a Mediset, a compartmentalized container that helps him remember the pills he needs to take each day. Another brings his service dog on a leash and an opossum that he found at his camp in the woods. The opossum rides on the man's shoulder before it is stowed for the service in a small carrier.

The notes from a Navajo flute calm the room and enfold us in mellow sound. Several voices read brief scriptures on today's theme: light coming into our lives and illuminating the path ahead. A hymn, with a new verse written for this occasion, links us to ages past; we sing of the weary way, but also of the night's brightening into dawn, giving birth to hope and promise. Welcoming words affirm the pulsing of the Spirit within every person. A parable tells of the moon and the stars as signs that, beyond what we can know and see, life is unending.

We are a multifaith group gathered from our many different spiritual journeys. Each of us brings our own experience and understanding of God, our particular traditions and expressions of the Holy. We are all here on the journey of recovery from mental illness, abuse, or addiction. We share a common desire for wholeness. We pray for one another and for family and friends who are not with us. We give thanks, speak of our pilgrimage, and seek strength.

At the heart of the service is a circle of quiet and sharing, in which anyone in the community is welcome to speak. A woman struggling with bipolar disorder reads a touching and wryly witty poem titled "Normal," after a town in Illinois by that name; she explains that she wrote the poem while wondering what it might be like to live in a place called Normal, and she draws applause when she observes that we all need to shape our own "normal." A second poet gives voice to the long night of separation from her family; her poem expresses how important are the little words of understanding that create pools of encouragement on her journey.

The work of the community is to hold each life in reverence, to honor the people who speak and support each other in this gathering of the broken and mending. Some speak briefly and with great clarity. Some share words of immense pain. Some struggle with guilt, loss, or grief. Some speak in voices so low that the words are unintelligible, or in language that is wandering and incoherent. But all are breathing in a quiet Spirit that gives and receives, understands and affirms, holds and accepts.

We compose a closing prayer together, each of us offering a word or sentence as we are able. A final song joins us in smiles and harmony, as a man of Hawaiian descent breaks out his ukulele. After the benediction— "Let us go and greet one another in peace"—there are hellos and conversations all around. No one is a stranger.

We head downstairs to the church's social lounge, where a long table is filled with food and drink, and smaller, round tables are set with place mats and silver. This is not just coffee and sheet cake; it is a feast of seafood and salads, plates of chicken kabobs, trays of fresh vegetables and fruit, baskets of hand-baked pita bread, and bowls of freshly made hummus. There are three different desserts, one rich with chocolate, a lemon tart, and a platter of homemade cookies.

Two men who have spent years on the street stop and glance at each other dubiously. One of them approaches Molly, the chef.

"Where's the meal for the mentally ill?" he asks.

Molly grins. "This is it."

"No," the man says, "this is stuff for important people. Ours must be somewhere else."

Molly assures him the food is for him and for everyone else. This is the feast to which all are welcome, the feast signaling that the providence of God includes us each—and especially those on the margins. And now the words and the simple ceremony that nourished our souls upstairs become words of conviviality shared along with the simple pleasure of enjoying a meal together.

The words we share with each other, the words we use to convey our concern and care, the words we offer to comfort a loved one or a stranger, the words we choose to express our suffering and point the way toward recovery—these words are medicine, too. The way we speak, the songs we sing, the rituals in which we engage, the colors we wear, the smile on our faces or the expressions of shared pain, the light in our eyes—all can help heal. When we bless a meal and when we "live" our words through acts of love and kindness, we give effect to the movement of the Spirit among us.

"God doesn't hate me," said Sylvie, embracing the full range of healing possible in her life. "The door will open," said Walter, envisioning his recovery during his hospitalization. "I'm grateful for caterpillars," said Josie, celebrating the promise of her own unfolding new future. "We can hold in our hands healing or guns. I choose healing," said Melika, recommitting herself to the practices of peace in a violent world.

Healing is possible. It takes place in the most difficult circumstances, on the streets, house by house, block by block, through the seven centuries in Geel, in war-torn Bosnia, whenever and wherever we approach with tenderness, speak with gentle truth, and act with love and kindness.

When Tom said, "Words are medicine, too," he did so within a context. He is a man of science, trained in the discipline of hypothesis, examination, testing, and diagnosis. He has seen many times over the improvements his patients have made with appropriate medications and treatment. He would urge that any soul suffering symptoms of a mental disorder have available the healing help of experienced and qualified physicians, nurses, psychologists, and counselors. Our understanding that "words are medicine, too" should not tempt us to think that faith can be a substitute for good medical care, or that a prayer is the same as a pill.

In the fullness of a person's recovery, spiritual language has its place alongside the vocabulary of science, medicine, therapy, and social work. The healing words of faith speak to us at the deepest levels of repair and renewal. The healing language of religion at its best fosters the life of the soul and promotes our wholeness as human beings. The language of the Spirit helps us name the ultimate sources of healing and well-being; it enables us to overcome our estrangement and rejoin the community of family, friends, and neighborhood. The central stories of salvation offer us a history within which we each can find our purpose. None of this—the words of scripture, our religious traditions, preaching, prayer, spiritual practice, and acts of faith— should replace effective medical treatment, but all can play an important role in healing.

One day I was walking with a man I'll call Roger when he suddenly stopped and pointed to a billboard advertising a special wolf exhibit at the Seattle zoo. It showed the fairy-tale figures of Little Red Riding Hood and a large gray wolf dressed up in Grandma's clothes.

"Do you see that wolf talking to that girl?" Roger said.

"Yes," I said.

"Do you hear what he's saying?"

"No."

"He's threatening her. We should call the police."

It was by no means Roger's first hallucinatory experience. He sometimes heard voices in the streets. He heard store-window mannequins talking behind their display windows. Radio announcers broadcast to the world what he ate for breakfast.

It was with some difficulty that I persuaded Roger there was no danger in the billboard. After some gentle conversation, he calmed down.

Roger was reluctant to talk about his symptoms. "People say you're crazy," he said. He glanced at the billboard again and then back to me, and an expression of wariness crossed his face. "Do you think I'm crazy?" he asked.

It's a question I've heard often. " 'Crazy' isn't a word I find useful," I said. "I don't think you're crazy. I think you've got something extraordinary going on. It can be frightening. You're a human being with a brain that doesn't always work. That's true for me too."

For centuries, our language has given us words that oversimplify and betray our lack of understanding, words that can sting and humiliate, words that convey stereotype and stigma. Crazy. Nuts. Cracked. Lunatic. These are not helpful words for understanding the medical condition of a brain disorder.

Our challenge in the twenty-first century is to shape a language of faith that speaks knowledgeably to the suffering of mental illness. We must search our ancient scriptures to find in them the vocabulary of healing, the words of love and understanding, the words of hospitality and companionship, the words of hope and grace. We are called to see illness not as a punishment or judgment, but as a sign of our finitude and vulnerability, and our need for one another in community. We are called to see mental illness in the light of a long human pilgrimage through the ages toward health and wholeness.

We have made a start. The national advocacy organization Pathways to Promise has helped develop mental illness networks in at least a dozen major Christian denominations. Members of Faithnet, an arm of the National Alliance on Mental Illness (NAMI), are working tirelessly to educate clergy and congregations, and to build a grassroots movement of people who understand the spiritual dimensions of mental illness. Mental illness ministry is emerging as a mission focus from Boston to Los Angeles, from Seattle to Miami, in large cities and small towns, in modest churches and megacongregations. We are being invited to share in healing conversations and care with our sisters and brothers who face disorders of the brain and disturbances in mood and thought. We are being called to a new understanding of behaviors that have caused so many among us to become isolated and estranged.

Within the larger discussions of science and religion, healing and faith, spirituality and mental health, the life of the soul in the course of mental illness is gaining new attention and focus.

The experience of mental illness can guide us to a fresh understanding of the complex gift that is the human brain. We have this remarkable organ so that we might join with the Spirit in creating a faithful world and an abundant life together. It is not simply for pursuing individual success or a solitary personal salvation that God gives us a brain. We—and our brains—are made for communication, companionship, collaboration, and community.

We are made to shape words into meaning, interpret tradition, create a new language of faith and belief. We are made for imagination and inspiration. We are made not just to know truth, but to become truth, to live authentically and honestly, to grow as souls with infinite value.

Mental illness derails us. It disrupts the deepest purpose of our being. Mental illness makes us wary of one another, erodes our confidence, disturbs and distorts our common life. It isolates us, tests us, and tempts us to give up our souls as lost. But the love of God and the power of the Spirit never break their connection to us and never cease caring for us.

This brain, which can become so disturbed, at its best gives us a capacity to co-create faithfulness, in partnership with God. We are made infinitely complex so that we might contribute to the continued shaping of the Word. God calls us to create scriptures, break new revelatory ground, and, with the help of the Spirit, shape a better world.

There is an essential power that persons suffering psychotic episodes experience—but in a distorted way, broken from the ground of community and self, and tenuously adrift from the counsel, comfort, and encouragement of the Spirit. Brain disorders conjure up extraordinary worlds of a unique kind, and many who live in those worlds believe that they are in the presence of pseudodivinities. Beyond the distortions of mental illness, however, is the hint of an important human truth: that we are called to spiritual imagination, to a faithful creativity, called to shape in every age and generation visions of wholeness and living communities of transcendent compassion, hope, and love.

God calls us to make out of our struggles new Edens; to become Abrahams and Sarahs on journeys from what is and has been to new destinations; to be in Exodus, to walk with each other through suffering to new habitations of promise and possibility. Illness cannot take from us our deepest identity. We are each of us anointed, touched with holy purpose, made to be bearers of the Spirit and full incarnations of God's love and grace in the world. We are the Acts that give birth to the sacred. Through our lives, in our strength and in our frailty, the Spirit moves, seeking ever to build communities of healing and growth for us all, souls in the hands of a tender God.

Epilogue

Terri, whom I first met while she was living on the steps of St. James Cathedral, made a courageous transition from the street to stability. She delighted in her apartment near St. James and was proud to serve as a eucharistic minister. She enjoyed her circle of friends and regular visits with her disabled son.

But then one day, her speech became slurred and it was hard for her to swallow. I went with her to see her neurologist, who had treated her seizures and tuberous sclerosis for years. He was puzzled. Terri's gait showed she was having some difficulty walking. The doctor ran her through a series of tests, focusing on her muscles, and finally gave her a disturbing diagnosis: amyotrophic lateral sclerosis (ALS), known as Lou Gehrig's disease, a progressive neuromuscular illness that weakens, and eventually destroys, motor neurons. It meant a gradual but inexorable deterioration of Terri's muscles. There was no cure.

In time, Terri could no longer swallow. She underwent an operation to install a feeding tube, but she continued to live at home and maintained her independence. When she grew weaker, she transferred to a nearby nursing home. There she spent her days slowly moving from room to room on her floor, bringing greetings and cards and small gifts to her fellow residents.

On Maundy Thursday, Terri asked me to buy a quart of chocolate milk and some cookies to leave with the priests at the rectory on Good Friday.

"It will help them keep up their strength through Holy Saturday and the Easter vigil and services," she explained.

I smiled and did as she asked.

It was the last time I visited her. On Easter Monday, Terri made her way to the nurses' station, returned a pencil she had borrowed, went back to her room, lay down, and died. On her bedside table, her Bible lay open to the book of Genesis, where this verse appeared: "Jacob drew up his feet into the bed and breathed his last and was gathered to his people" (Gen. 49:33).

We celebrated a funeral mass the next week at noon, a worship hour especially dear to Terri. Just as we were leaving the cathedral, the procession paused. For a moment, the casket rested over the cathedral crypt, the burial place of the bishops of the archdiocese. Father Michael Ryan raised his eyes to the dome of the cathedral, where light streams in from a great circle open to the sky, and proclaimed a final high blessing: The gates of heaven are open. The angels sing welcome, and the whole host and company of God's people gone before us greet our sister Terri with great joy.

I could see, by the eye of faith, a tender hand reaching down toward Terri to share with her the continuing journey, and a cloud of witnesses such as Father Ryan described. Among them was my long-ago friend Sterling Hayden, standing beside the Gerasene whom Jesus healed, surrounded by a vast community of souls, once alone and now gathered in a glorious and great Love.

Acknowledgments

This book would not have been written without David's encouragement and partnership in writing. It has been an extraordinarily shared experience, one in which I have been able to explore and bring to word feelings, ideas, and beliefs that David midwifed with great sensitivity, patience, and thoughtfulness. He listened deeply, clarified the vague and cloudy, added his own rich wisdom, and gently and persistently carried away the dross that accumulates in refining a sentence, a paragraph, a chapter and book. I owe an equally uncountable debt to Barb, who has supported me in living and telling the healing story. Barb's love and presence, her soul and grace and faithfulness, have embraced me in the most painful hours and helped me find the deepest joys. I cannot begin to say thanks enough to Barb and to Kelsey, Sam, and Max for their care and understanding, and for being *home*. To the family—Mom and Dad, Kris, Rob and Laurie, to the clan Rennebohm and the clan Bennett, thank you for your nurturing, adventurousness, humor, and help.

My faith journey has benefited from the gifts of mentors and colleagues: Lee Longrie, Dick Preis, David Maitland; the faculty at Chicago Theological Seminary and my fellow student John Bodwell; pastors Tom Dipko and Frank Kelsey; Clinical Pastoral Education supervisor Dick Flowers; Professors Archie Smith, Valerie DeMarinis, and Francis Bauer at the Pacific School of Religion and the Graduate Theological Union; Rev. Patrick Howell, Chaplains Vivian Bowden, Sue Gosline, Dick Lutz, and the board members of the

Mental Health Chaplaincy; Nancy Smith and the Plymouth Healing Communities; the people of Christ Church United in Lowell, Mass., and Pilgrim Church in Seattle; the congregations and staff of Plymouth and Prospect Congregational Churches, the Church Council of Greater Seattle, and the many churches and individuals who have made the Chaplaincy possible. Communities form us each, and I am grateful for all who have helped shape a lifetime of ministry.

A wider community of colleagues in human service, social work, psychology, psychiatry, and medicine has also contributed mightily to my learning. Sue Eastgard, MSW, and Drs. David Avery, Sharon Farmer, and Andrew Borland provided important guidance. In particular, I want to thank Ken Kraybill for his invitation to become part of the work of Health Care for the Homeless and for his collaboration in developing the practices of companionship and relational outreach and engagement.

Duane and Kay Glasscock and Gunnar Christiansen introduced me to the work of NAMI, the National Alliance on Mental Illness. Bob Dell has shared generously from his experience with the United Church of Christ Mental Illness Network and the work of Pathways to Promise.

The Chaplaincy has also enjoyed an international collegiality. I am grateful to Dr. Dada Maglajlić for the opportunity to participate in the annual Symposium on Spirituality and Social Work in Dubrovnik, Croatia, to Dr. Jim Withers for the invitation to join the annual meetings of the International Street Medicine Symposium, and to Claus Wagner in Berlin. I am grateful to all who have broadened my perspectives.

I want especially to thank three healers: the Reverend Leonard Gibbs, director of the Lowell Pastoral Counseling Center, (the late) therapist Irv Goldberg, PhD, and Abby Franklin, MD, holding in their care body, mind, and spirit, the whole person.

Finally, I offer thanks to the students and laity who have participated in the life of the Chaplaincy, and to the sisters and brothers with whom I have shared the journey on the streets and in the hospital and in the community. You are the day-to-day base community in which *Souls in the Hands of a Tender God* is rooted.

Craig Rennebohm

I want to thank Craig for living the life and doing the work that make this book a compelling testament, and for being a creative, inspiring, indefatigable, and always good-humored writing partner. I am also grateful to Nancy Jacobs for her support and patience, and for providing a beautiful workspace within our home where creative ideas take shape readily.

David Paul

We both are indebted to our agent, Judy Mikalonis of the Andrea Hurst Agency, who helped us craft a persuasive book proposal and found a home for our fledgling manuscript. Judy's tireless enthusiasm and faith buoyed our spirits along the road to publication. We acknowledge also the input of Elizabeth Frost-Knappman, Andrea Somberg, and Stephanie Rostan, whose early comments on our work helped point us in the right direction.

Finally, we are grateful for the skilled editorial work of Amy Caldwell and Tracy Ahlquist of Beacon Press, who were quick to "get it" about the message of this book. They and their able production team have made the process of moving the manuscript to publication a breeze.

Craig Rennebohm and David Paul

Appendixes

Appendix A: A Call to Healing Ministry

The experience of mental illness invites us to acknowledge our vulnerability and brokenness, our need for others and for help. When our minds and brains are malfunctioning, we need community and the love and care of others in order to be well. We know that we are not sufficient in ourselves, but have life and hope because we are held by a great tenderness and in a Spirit of deep healing and grace.

The numbers of souls in need of help are great. A tithe of humanity, a quarter of our families, wait for ministry. In and among the neighbors of every congregation are individuals seeking healing and recovery from mental illness and families seeking support for a challenging journey.

Too often the life of the church has been silent on matters of mental illness. Those who suffer find little welcome. Ignorance, stigma, embarrassment, and shame keep a curtain drawn upon the need. Souls remain unvisited in home and hospital. Providers of spiritual care and psychiatric services rarely converse with each other, or even meet.

Yet God has not abandoned us who suffer deeply in brain, in mood and thought, and in profound struggles of anxiousness and relationship.

The Spirit is ever active, welcoming us with love into lives of wholeness, encouraging us to understand our vulnerabilities and brokenness, and calling us to share healing journeys with one another in communities of care. Mental health ministry understands that the brain can malfunction, can be in distress and disorder and in need of healing. Mental health ministry offers personal spiritual care supportive of recovery and encouragement for families who face illness. Mental health ministry shares the journey and acts to make care more effective and readily available.

Ministries with people facing mental illness offer education, companionship, family support, and public witness, thereby building caring neighborhoods and healing community.

Let us begin our educational efforts by inviting those who experience mental illness and their families to speak in our midst. Let us talk with those who have trained and practiced in the field of psychiatry and mental health. Let us hear from spiritual caregivers who have worked most closely with mental illness. Let us explore and review what local congregations and networks of churches have developed. Let us make a special effort each year during Mental Illness Awareness Week in October and Mental Health Month in May to highlight our care and concern.

Let us prepare ourselves to offer companionship, provide hospitality, come alongside, listen to, and accompany our fellow human beings who face the journey with mental illness. Let at least one of us be especially available when the community gathers, to offer a ministry of presence with those who come in distress or linger alone on the edges of our life together. Let us provide intentional one-to-one support programs, a weekly Bible study, a peer spiritual support group, and opportunities to explore together spiritual practices that are supportive of recovery. Let us form small teams of community companions committed to spending time each week at meal programs, drop-in centers, shelters, and residences where fellowship and human company are most needed. Let us grow in our companionship capacities that we may serve as Good Samaritans reaching out to those most hidden and isolated in our communities.

Let us offer encouragement to families facing mental illness. Let us help by hosting a NAMI "Family to Family" program; providing a regular meeting time for a family support group; organizing a spiritual support group with families, spouses, or siblings; or developing support for a mentally ill parent and his or her children.

Let us develop from our experience of direct service, and in collaboration with other congregations and community groups, a strong public witness in support of an effective and easily accessible community mental health system. Let us work to ensure timely and proactive outreach when a person begins to suffer. Let us advocate for continuing research and the development of appropriate medications and treatment. Let us make sufficient hospital and clinic resources available to all. Let us build the range of supported and affordable convalescent housing needed to provide safe homes for our sisters and brothers so that no one facing mental illness is left uncared for on our streets or in our jails and prisons.

And let those of us who experience these far edges of existence in our illness be also of service. Let us share with others what we have learned of brokenness and healing, vulnerability and salvation. Let those of us who have faced depression, battled mania, been subject to hallucinations or delusions, fought paranoia, wrestled with great fears and anxiety, lived through horrific trauma, and struggled with alcohol and drugs let us honor recovery's calling and take our responsible part in creating caring community, each of us as our healing will permit.

Let us be in healing ministry together, following the ways that make for growth, wholeness, and peace.

Appendix B: Books

Boisen, Anton. *The Exploration of the Inner World: A Study of Mental Disorder and Religious Experience.* Chicago and New York: Willett, Clark, 1936; reissued Philadelphia: University of Pennsylvania Press, 1971.

Boisen, Anton. *Out of the Depths: An Autobiographical Study of Mental Disorder and Religious Experience.* New York: Harper and Brothers, 1960.

Bhugra, Dinesh, ed. *Psychiatry and Religion: Consensus and Controversies.* Oxford, UK: Routledge, 1996.

Damasio, Antonio. *Looking for Spinoza: Joy, Sorrow, and the Feeling Brain.* New York: Harcourt, 2003.

Galanter, Marc. *Spirituality and the Healthy Mind: Science, Therapy, and the Need for Personal Meaning.* New York: Oxford University Press, 2005.

Govig, Stewart D. *In the Shadow of Our Steeples: Pastoral Presence for Families Coping with Mental Illness.* Binghamton, NY: Haworth Press, 1999.

Govig, Stewart D. *Souls Are Made of Endurance: Survival of Mental Illness in the Family.* Binghamton, NY: Haworth Press, 1994.

Gregg-Schroeder, Susan. *In the Shadow of God's Wings: Grace in the Midst of Depression.* Nashville, TN: Upper Room Books, 1997.

Howell, Patrick J. *Reducing the Storm to a Whisper.* Chicago: Thomas More Press, 1985.

Howell, Patrick. *A Spiritguide: As Sure as the Dawn through Times of Darkness.* Lanham, MD: Sheed & Ward, 1996.

Kenig, Sylvia. *Who Plays? Who Pays? Who Cares? A Case Study in Applied Sociology, Political Economy and the Community Mental Health Centers Movement.* Amityville, NY: Baywood, 1992.

Koenig, Harold. *The Healing Power of Faith: How Belief and Prayer Can Help You Triumph Over Disease.* New York: Simon & Schuster, 2001.

Nouwen, Henri J. M. *The Wounded Healer: Ministry in Contemporary Society.* Garden City, NJ: Doubleday, 1972.

Oates, Wayne E. *The Religious Care of the Psychiatric Patient.* Philadelphia: Westminster Press, 1978.

Torrey, E. Fuller. *Nowhere to Go: The Tragic Odyssey of the Homeless Mentally Ill.* New York: Harper and Row, 1988.

Zohar, Danah, with I. N. Marshall. *The Quantum Self.* New York: Morrow, 1990.

Appendix C: Organizations

National Alliance on Mental Illness (NAMI)

www.nami.org

The United States' largest grassroots mental-health organization dedicated to improving the lives of persons living with serious mental illness and their families. Fifty state-level affiliates plus the District of Columbia, Puerto Rico, and more than twelve hundred local affiliates.

NAMI FaithNet (faithnet.nami.org), is a NAMI-based network that offers support to those with serious mental illness and their families, educates clergy and congregations about mental illness, and encourages faith communities to help all who are affected by mental illness. NAMI FaithNet sponsors an e-mail support network and distributes an e-mail newsletter to subscribers.

Pathways to Promise

www.pathways2promise.org

An interfaith technical assistance and resource center offering liturgical and educational materials, program models, and networking information to promote a caring ministry among people with mental illness and their families.

Specific faith-based mental illness ministries, including many Christian and Jewish organizations sponsoring mental health ministry and advocacy programs at the national level, are listed, with links to their Web sites, at www.pathways2promise.org/resources/faithgroup.htm.

Mental Health Ministries

www.mentalhealthministries.net

Resource center begun as an outreach program of the California-Pacific Conference of the United Methodist Church and headed by the Reverend Susan Gregg-Schroeder, offering videos, books, and workshops.

Mental Health Chaplaincy

www.mentalhealthchaplain.org

Author Craig Rennebohm's nonprofit organization, established in Seattle to serve the homeless mentally ill locally, and now offering training workshops, books, and other materials to congregations and healthcare institutions engaged in mental health ministry.

National Health Care for the Homeless Council (HCH)

www.nhchc.org

Service organization working to improve the health of homeless people and advocate for housing, healthcare, and adequate incomes for everyone; ninety-five local and regional affiliates.

Mental Health America (formerly the National Mental Health Association)

www.mentalhealthamerica.net

Major national nonprofit organization dedicated to helping people live mentally healthier lives; 320 local and regional affiliates.